MW00581102

The Book of

PSALMS

ISBN 13: 978-1-5154-4096-3

The Book of

PSALMS

PSALM 1

1:1 Blessed [is] the man that walketh not in the counsel of the ungodly, nor standeth in the way of sinners, nor sitteth in the seat of the scornful. 1:2 But his delight [is] in the law of the LORD; and in his law doth he meditate day and night. 1:3 And he shall be like a tree planted by the rivers of water, that bringeth forth his fruit in his season; his leaf also shall not wither; and whatsoever he doeth shall prosper. 1:4 The ungodly [are] not so: but [are] like the chaff which the wind driveth away. 1:5 Therefore the ungodly shall not stand in the judgment, nor sinners in the congregation of the righteous. 1:6 For the LORD knoweth the way of the righteous: but the way of the ungodly shall perish.

PSALM 2

2:1 Why do the heathen rage, and the people imagine a vain thing? 2:2 The kings of the earth set themselves, and the rulers take counsel together, against the LORD, and against his anointed, [saying], 2:3 Let us break their bands asunder, and cast away their cords from us. 2:4 He that sitteth in the heavens shall laugh: the Lord shall have them in derision. 2:5 Then shall he speak unto them in his wrath, and vex them in his sore displeasure. 2:6 Yet have I set my king upon my holy hill of Zion. 2:7 I will declare the decree: the LORD hath said unto me, Thou [art] my Son; this day have I begotten thee. 2:8 Ask of me, and I shall give [thee] the heathen [for] thine inheritance, and the uttermost parts of the earth [for] thy possession. 2:9 Thou shalt break them with a rod of iron; thou shalt dash them in pieces like a potter's vessel. 2:10 Be wise now therefore, O ye kings: be instructed, ye judges of the earth. 2:11 Serve the LORD with fear, and rejoice with trembling. 2:12 Kiss the Son, lest he be angry, and ye perish [from] the way, when his wrath is kindled but a little. Blessed [are] all they that put their trust in him.

PSALM 3

A PSALM of David, when he fled from Absalom his son. 3:1 LORD, how are they increased that trouble me! many [are] they that rise up against me. 3:2

Many [there be] which say of my soul, [There is] no help for him in God. Selah. 3:3 But thou, O LORD, [art] a shield for me; my glory, and the lifter up of mine head. 3:4 I cried unto the LORD with my voice, and he heard me out of his holy hill. Selah. 3:5 I laid me down and slept; I awaked; for the LORD sustained me. 3:6 I will not be afraid of ten thousands of people, that have set [themselves] against me round about. 3:7 Arise, O LORD; save me, O my God: for thou hast smitten all mine enemies [upon] the cheek bone; thou hast broken the teeth of the ungodly. 3:8 Salvation [belongeth] unto the LORD: thy blessing [is] upon thy people. Selah.

PSALM 4
To the chief Musician on Neginoth, A PSALM of David. 4:1 Hear me when I call, O God of my righteousness: thou hast enlarged me [when I was] in distress; have mercy upon me, and hear my prayer. 4:2 O ye sons of men, how long [will ye turn] my glory into shame? [how long] will ye love vanity, [and] seek after leasing? Selah. 4:3 But know that the LORD hath set apart him that is godly for himself: the LORD will hear when I call unto him. 4:4 Stand in awe, and sin not: commune with your own heart upon your bed, and be still. Selah. 4:5 Offer the sacrifices of righteousness, and put your trust in the LORD. 4:6 [There be] many that say, Who will shew us [any] good? LORD, lift thou up the light of thy countenance upon us. 4:7 Thou hast put gladness in my heart, more than in the time [that] their corn and their wine increased. 4:8 I will both lay me down in peace, and sleep: for thou, LORD, only makest me dwell in safety.

PSALM 5
To the chief Musician upon Nehiloth, A PSALM of David. 5:1 Give ear to my words, O LORD, consider my meditation. 5:2 Hearken unto the voice of my cry, my King, and my God: for unto thee will I pray. 5:3 My voice shalt thou hear in the morning, O LORD; in the morning will I direct [my prayer] unto thee, and will look up. 5:4 For thou [art] not a God that hath pleasure in wickedness: neither shall evil dwell with thee. 5:5 The foolish shall not

stand in thy sight: thou hatest all workers of iniquity. 5:6 Thou shalt destroy them that speak leasing: the LORD will abhor the bloody and deceitful man. 5:7 But as for me, I will come [into] thy house in the multitude of thy mercy: [and] in thy fear will I worship toward thy holy temple. 5:8 Lead me, O LORD, in thy righteousness because of mine enemies; make thy way straight before my face. 5:9 For [there is] no faithfulness in their mouth; their inward part [is] very wickedness; their throat [is] an open sepulchre; they flatter with their tongue. 5:10 Destroy thou them, O God; let them fall by their own counsels; cast them out in the multitude of their transgressions; for they have rebelled against thee. 5:11 But let all those that put their trust in thee rejoice: let them ever shout for joy, because thou defendest them: let them also that love thy name be joyful in thee. 5:12 For thou, LORD, wilt bless the righteous; with favour wilt thou compass him as [with] a shield.

PSALM 6
To the chief Musician on Neginoth upon Sheminith, A PSALM of David. 6:1 O LORD, rebuke me not in thine anger, neither chasten me in thy hot displeasure. 6:2 Have mercy upon me, O LORD; for I [am] weak: O LORD, heal me; for my bones are vexed. 6:3 My soul is also sore vexed: but thou, O LORD, how long? 6:4 Return, O LORD, deliver my soul: oh save me for thy mercies' sake. 6:5 For in death [there is] no remembrance of thee: in the grave who shall give thee thanks? 6:6 I am weary with my groaning; all the night make I my bed to swim; I water my couch with my tears. 6:7 Mine eye is consumed because of grief; it waxeth old because of all mine enemies. 6:8 Depart from me, all ye workers of iniquity; for the LORD hath heard the voice of my weeping. 6:9 The LORD hath heard my supplication; the LORD will receive my prayer. 6:10 Let all mine enemies be ashamed and sore vexed: let them return [and] be ashamed suddenly.

PSALM 7
Shiggaion of David, which he sang unto the LORD, concerning the words of Cush the Benjamite. 7:1 O LORD my God, in thee do I put my trust: save

me from all them that persecute me, and deliver me: 7:2 Lest he tear my soul like a lion, rending [it] in pieces, while [there is] none to deliver. 7:3 O LORD my God, if I have done this; if there be iniquity in my hands; 7:4 If I have rewarded evil unto him that was at peace with me; (yea, I have delivered him that without cause is mine enemy:) 7:5 Let the enemy persecute my soul, and take [it]; yea, let him tread down my life upon the earth, and lay mine honour in the dust. Selah. 7:6 Arise, O LORD, in thine anger, lift up thyself because of the rage of mine enemies: and awake for me [to] the judgment [that] thou hast commanded. 7:7 So shall the congregation of the people compass thee about: for their sakes therefore return thou on high. 7:8 The LORD shall judge the people: judge me, O LORD, according to my righteousness, and according to mine integrity [that is] in me. 7:9 Oh let the wickedness of the wicked come to an end; but establish the just: for the righteous God trieth the hearts and reins. 7:10 My defence [is] of God, which saveth the upright in heart. 7:11 God judgeth the righteous, and God is angry [with the wicked] every day. 7:12 If he turn not, he will whet his sword; he hath bent his bow, and made it ready. 7:13 He hath also prepared for him the instruments of death; he ordaineth his arrows against the persecutors. 7:14 Behold, he travaileth with iniquity, and hath conceived mischief, and brought forth falsehood. 7:15 He made a pit, and digged it, and is fallen into the ditch [which] he made. 7:16 His mischief shall return upon his own head, and his violent dealing shall come down upon his own pate. 7:17 I will praise the LORD according to his righteousness: and will sing praise to the name of the LORD most high.

PSALM 8

To the chief Musician upon Gittith, A PSALM of David. 8:1 O LORD our Lord, how excellent [is] thy name in all the earth! who hast set thy glory above the heavens. 8:2 Out of the mouth of babes and sucklings hast thou ordained strength because of thine enemies, that thou mightest still the enemy and the avenger. 8:3 When I consider thy heavens, the work of thy fingers, the moon and the stars, which thou hast ordained; 8:4 What is man, that thou art mindful of him? and the son of man, that thou visitest him? 8:5 For thou hast made him a little lower than the angels, and hast crowned him with glory and honour. 8:6 Thou madest him to have dominion over the works of thy hands; thou hast put all [things] under his feet: 8:7 All sheep and oxen, yea, and the beasts of the field; 8:8 The fowl of the air, and the fish of the sea, [and whatsoever] passeth through the paths of the seas. 8:9 O LORD our Lord, how excellent [is] thy name in all the earth!

PSALM 9

To the chief Musician upon Muthlabben, A PSALM of David. 9:1 I will praise [thee], O LORD, with my whole heart; I will shew forth all thy marvellous works. 9:2 I will be glad and rejoice in thee: I will sing praise to thy name, O thou most High. 9:3 When mine enemies are turned back, they shall fall and perish at thy presence. 9:4 For thou hast maintained my right and my cause; thou satest in the throne judging right. 9:5 Thou hast rebuked the heathen, thou hast destroyed the wicked, thou hast put out their name for ever and ever. 9:6 O thou enemy, destructions are come to a perpetual end: and thou hast destroyed cities; their memorial is perished with them. 9:7 But the LORD shall endure for ever: he hath prepared his throne for judgment. 9:8 And he shall judge the world in righteousness, he shall minister judgment to the people in uprightness. 9:9 The LORD also will be a refuge for the oppressed, a refuge in times of trouble. 9:10 And they that know thy name will put their trust in thee: for thou, LORD, hast not forsaken them that seek thee. 9:11 Sing praises to the LORD, which dwelleth in Zion: declare among the people his doings. 9:12 When he maketh inquisition for blood, he remembereth them: he forgetteth not the cry of the humble. 9:13 Have mercy upon me, O LORD; consider my trouble [which I suffer] of them that hate me, thou that liftest me up from the gates of death: 9:14 That I may shew forth all thy praise in the gates of the daughter of Zion: I will rejoice in thy salvation. 9:15 The heathen are sunk down in the pit [that] they made: in the net which they hid is their own foot taken. 9:16 The LORD is known [by] the judgment [which] he executeth: the wicked is snared in the work of his own hands. Higgaion. Selah. 9:17 The wicked shall be turned into hell, [and] all the nations that forget God. 9:18 For the needy shall not alway be forgotten: the expectation of the poor shall [not] perish for ever. 9:19 Arise, O LORD; let not man prevail: let the heathen be judged in thy sight. 9:20 Put them in fear, O LORD: [that] the nations may know themselves [to be but] men. Selah.

PSALM 10

10:1 Why standest thou afar off, O LORD? [why] hidest thou [thyself] in times of trouble? 10:2 The wicked in [his] pride doth persecute the poor: let them be taken in the devices that they have imagined. 10:3 For the wicked boasteth of his heart's desire, and blesseth the covetous, [whom] the LORD abhorreth. 10:4 The wicked, through the pride of his countenance, will not seek [after God]: God [is] not in all his thoughts. 10:5 His ways are always grievous; thy judgments [are] far above out of his sight: [as for] all his enemies, he puffeth at them. 10:6 He hath said in his heart, I shall not be moved: for [I shall] never [be] in adversity. 10:7 His mouth is full of cursing and deceit and fraud: under his tongue [is] mischief and vanity. 10:8 He sitteth in the lurking places of the villages: in the secret places doth he murder the innocent: his eyes are privily set against the poor. 10:9 He lieth in wait secretly as a lion in his den: he lieth in wait to catch the poor: he doth catch the poor, when he draweth him into his net. 10:10 He croucheth, [and] humbleth himself, that the poor may fall by his strong ones. 10:11 He hath said in his heart, God hath forgotten: he hideth his face; he will never see [it]. 10:12 Arise, O LORD; O God, lift up thine hand: forget not the humble. 10:13 Wherefore doth the wicked contemn God? he hath said in his heart, Thou wilt not require [it]. 10:14 Thou hast seen [it]; for thou beholdest mischief and spite, to requite [it] with thy hand: the poor committeth himself unto thee; thou art the helper of the fatherless. 10:15 Break thou the arm of the wicked and the evil [man]: seek out his wickedness [till] thou find none. 10:16 The LORD [is] King for ever and ever: the heathen are perished out of his land. 10:17 LORD, thou hast heard the desire of the humble: thou wilt prepare their heart, thou wilt cause thine ear to hear: 10:18 To judge the fatherless and the oppressed, that the man of the earth may no more oppress.

PSALM 11

To the chief Musician, [A PSALM] of David. 11:1 In the LORD put I my trust: how say ye to my soul, Flee [as] a bird to your mountain? 11:2 For, lo, the wicked bend [their] bow, they make ready their arrow upon the string, that they may privily shoot at the upright in heart. 11:3 If the foundations be destroyed, what can the righteous do? 11:4 The LORD [is] in his holy temple, the LORD's throne [is] in heaven: his eyes behold, his eyelids try, the children of men. 11:5 The LORD trieth the righteous: but the wicked and him that loveth violence his soul hateth. 11:6 Upon the wicked he shall rain snares, fire and brimstone, and an horrible tempest: [this shall be] the portion of their cup. 11:7 For the righteous LORD loveth righteousness; his countenance doth behold the upright.

PSALM 12

To the chief Musician upon Sheminith, A PSALM of David. 12:1 Help, LORD; for the godly man ceaseth; for the faithful fail from among the children of men. 12:2 They speak vanity every one with his neighbour: [with] flattering li[and] with a double heart do they speak. 12:3 The LORD shall cut off all flattering lips, [and] the tongue that speaketh proud things: 12:4 Who have said, With our tongue will we prevail; our li[are] our own: who [is] lord over us? 12:5 For the oppression of the poor, for the sighing of the needy, now will I arise, saith the LORD; I will set [him] in safety [from him that] puffeth at him. 12:6 The words of the LORD [are] pure words: [as] silver tried in a furnace of earth, purified seven times. 12:7 Thou shalt keep them, O LORD, thou shalt preserve them from this generation for ever. 12:8 The wicked walk on every side, when the vilest men are exalted.

PSALM 13

To the chief Musician, A PSALM of David. 13:1 How long wilt thou forget me, O LORD? for ever? how long wilt thou hide thy face from me? 13:2 How long shall I take counsel in my soul, [having] sorrow in my heart daily? how long shall mine enemy be exalted over me? 13:3 Consider [and] hear me, O LORD my God: lighten mine eyes, lest I sleep the [sleep of] death; 13:4 Lest mine enemy say, I have prevailed against him; [and] those that trouble me rejoice when I am moved. 13:5 But I have trusted in thy mercy; my heart shall rejoice in thy salvation. 13:6 I will sing unto the LORD, because he hath dealt bountifully with me.

PSALM 14

To the chief Musician, [A PSALM] of David. 14:1 The fool hath said in his heart, [There is] no God. They are corrupt, they have done abominable works, [there is] none that doeth good. 14:2 The LORD looked down from heaven upon the children of men, to see if there were any that did understand, [and] seek God. 14:3 They are all gone aside, they are [all] together become filthy: [there is] none that doeth good, no, not one. 14:4 Have all the workers of iniquity no knowledge? who eat up my people [as] they eat bread, and call not upon the LORD. 14:5 There were they in great fear: for God [is] in the generation of the righteous. 14:6 Ye have shamed the counsel of the poor, because the LORD [is] his refuge. 14:7 Oh that the salvation of Israel [were come] out of Zion! when the LORD bringeth back the captivity of his people, Jacob shall rejoice, [and] Israel shall be glad.

PSALM 15

A PSALM of David. 15:1 LORD, who shall abide in thy tabernacle? who shall dwell in thy holy hill? 15:2 He that walketh uprightly, and worketh righteousness, and speaketh the truth in his heart. 15:3 [He that] backbiteth not with his tongue, nor doeth evil to his neighbour, nor taketh up a reproach against his neighbour. 15:4 In whose eyes a vile person is contemned; but he honoureth them that fear the LORD. [He that] sweareth to [his own] hurt, and changeth not. 15:5 [He that] putteth not out his money to usury, nor taketh reward against the innocent. He that doeth these [things] shall never be moved.

PSALM 16

Michtam of David. 16:1 Preserve me, O God: for in thee do I put my trust. 16:2 [O my soul], thou hast said unto the LORD, Thou [art] my Lord: my goodness [extendeth] not to thee; 16:3 [But] to the saints that [are] in the earth, and [to] the excellent, in whom [is] all my delight. 16:4 Their sorrows shall be multiplied [that] hasten [after] another [god]: their drink offerings of blood will I not offer, nor take up their names into my lips. 16:5 The LORD [is] the portion of mine inheritance and of my cup: thou maintainest my lot. 16:6 The lines are fallen unto me in pleasant [places]; yea, I have a goodly heritage. 16:7 I will bless the LORD, who hath given me counsel: my reins also instruct me in the night seasons. 16:8 I have set the LORD always before me: because [he is] at my right hand, I shall not be moved. 16:9 Therefore my heart is glad, and my glory rejoiceth: my flesh also shall rest in hope. 16:10 For thou wilt not leave my soul in hell; neither wilt thou suffer thine Holy One to see corruption. 16:11 Thou wilt shew me the path of life: in thy presence [is] fulness of joy; at thy right hand [there are] pleasures for evermore.

PSALM 17

A Prayer of David. 17:1 Hear the right, O LORD, attend unto my cry, give ear unto my prayer, [that goeth] not out of feigned lips. 17:2 Let my sentence come forth from thy presence; let thine eyes behold the things that are equal. 17:3 Thou hast proved mine heart; thou hast visited [me] in the night; thou hast tried me, [and] shalt find nothing; I am purposed [that] my mouth shall not transgress. 17:4 Concerning the works of men, by the word of thy liI have kept [me from] the paths of the destroyer. 17:5 Hold up my goings in thy paths, [that] my footsteslip not. 17:6 I have called upon thee, for thou wilt hear me, O God: incline thine ear unto me, [and hear] my speech. 17:7 Shew thy marvellous lovingkindness, O thou that savest by thy right hand them which put their trust [in thee] from those that rise up [against them]. 17:8

Keep me as the apple of the eye, hide me under the shadow of thy wings, 17:9 From the wicked that oppress me, [from] my deadly enemies, [who] compass me about. 17:10 They are inclosed in their own fat: with their mouth they speak proudly. 17:11 They have now compassed us in our steps: they have set their eyes bowing down to the earth; 17:12 Like as a lion [that] is greedy of his prey, and as it were a young lion lurking in secret places. 17:13 Arise, O LORD, disappoint him, cast him down: deliver my soul from the wicked, [which is] thy sword: 17:14 From men [which are] thy hand, O LORD, from men of the world, [which have] their portion in [this] life, and whose belly thou fillest with thy hid [treasure]: they are full of children, and leave the rest of their [substance] to their babes. 17:15 As for me, I will behold thy face in righteousness: I shall be satisfied, when I awake, with thy likeness.

PSALM 18

To the chief Musician, [A PSALM] of David, the servant of the LORD, who spake unto the LORD the words of this song in the day [that] the LORD delivered him from the hand of all his enemies, and from the hand of Saul: And he said, 18:1 I will love thee, O LORD, my strength. 18:2 The LORD [is] my rock, and my fortress, and my deliverer; my God, my strength, in whom I will trust; my buckler, and the horn of my salvation, [and] my high tower. 18:3 I will call upon the LORD, [who is worthy] to be praised: so shall I be saved from mine enemies. 18:4 The sorrows of death compassed me, and the floods of ungodly men made me afraid. 18:5 The sorrows of hell compassed me about: the snares of death prevented me. 18:6 In my distress I called upon the LORD, and cried unto my God: he heard my voice out of his temple, and my cry came before him, [even] into his ears. 18:7 Then the earth shook and trembled; the foundations also of the hills moved and were shaken, because he was wroth. 18:8 There went up a smoke out of his nostrils, and fire out of his mouth devoured: coals were kindled by it. 18:9 He bowed the heavens also, and came down: and darkness [was] under his feet. 18:10 And he rode upon a cherub, and did fly: yea, he did fly upon the

wings of the wind. 18:11 He made darkness his secret place; his pavilion
round about him [were] dark waters [and] thick clouds of the skies. 18:12 At
the brightness [that was] before him his thick clouds passed, hail [stones] and
coals of fire. 18:13 The LORD also thundered in the heavens, and the
Highest gave his voice; hail [stones] and coals of fire. 18:14 Yea, he sent out
his arrows, and scattered them; and he shot out lightnings, and discomfited
them. 18:15 Then the channels of waters were seen, and the foundations of
the world were discovered at thy rebuke, O LORD, at the blast of the breath
of thy nostrils. 18:16 He sent from above, he took me, he drew me out of
many waters. 18:17 He delivered me from my strong enemy, and from them
which hated me: for they were too strong for me. 18:18 They prevented me
in the day of my calamity: but the LORD was my stay. 18:19 He brought me
forth also into a large place; he delivered me, because he delighted in me.
18:20 The LORD rewarded me according to my righteousness; according to
the cleanness of my hands hath he recompensed me. 18:21 For I have kept
the ways of the LORD, and have not wickedly departed from my God. 18:22
For all his judgments [were] before me, and I did not put away his statutes
from me. 18:23 I was also upright before him, and I kept myself from mine
iniquity. 18:24 Therefore hath the LORD recompensed me according to my
righteousness, according to the cleanness of my hands in his eyesight. 18:25
With the merciful thou wilt shew thyself merciful; with an upright man thou
wilt shew thyself upright; 18:26 With the pure thou wilt shew thyself pure;
and with the froward thou wilt shew thyself froward. 18:27 For thou wilt save
the afflicted people; but wilt bring down high looks. 18:28 For thou wilt light
my candle: the LORD my God will enlighten my darkness. 18:29 For by thee
I have run through a troop; and by my God have I leaped over a wall. 18:30
[As for] God, his way [is] perfect: the word of the LORD is tried: he [is] a
buckler to all those that trust in him. 18:31 For who [is] God save the
LORD? or who [is] a rock save our God? 18:32 [It is] God that girdeth me
with strength, and maketh my way perfect. 18:33 He maketh my feet like
hinds' [feet], and setteth me upon my high places. 18:34 He teacheth my
hands to war, so that a bow of steel is broken by mine arms. 18:35 Thou hast

also given me the shield of thy salvation: and thy right hand hath holden me
up, and thy gentleness hath made me great. 18:36 Thou hast enlarged my
steunder me, that my feet did not slip. 18:37 I have pursued mine enemies,
and overtaken them: neither did I turn again till they were consumed. 18:38
I have wounded them that they were not able to rise: they are fallen under
my feet. 18:39 For thou hast girded me with strength unto the battle: thou
hast subdued under me those that rose up against me. 18:40 Thou hast also
given me the necks of mine enemies; that I might destroy them that hate me.
18:41 They cried, but [there was] none to save [them: even] unto the LORD,
but he answered them not. 18:42 Then did I beat them small as the dust
before the wind: I did cast them out as the dirt in the streets. 18:43 Thou
hast delivered me from the strivings of the people; [and] thou hast made me
the head of the heathen: a people [whom] I have not known shall serve me.
18:44 As soon as they hear of me, they shall obey me: the strangers shall
submit themselves unto me. 18:45 The strangers shall fade away, and be
afraid out of their close places. 18:46 The LORD liveth; and blessed [be] my
rock; and let the God of my salvation be exalted. 18:47 [It is] God that
avengeth me, and subdueth the people under me. 18:48 He delivereth me
from mine enemies: yea, thou liftest me up above those that rise up against
me: thou hast delivered me from the violent man. 18:49 Therefore will I give
thanks unto thee, O LORD, among the heathen, and sing praises unto thy
name. 18:50 Great deliverance giveth he to his king; and sheweth mercy to
his anointed, to David, and to his seed for evermore.

PSALM 19

To the chief Musician, A PSALM of David. 19:1 The heavens declare the
glory of God; and the firmament sheweth his handywork. 19:2 Day unto day
uttereth speech, and night unto night sheweth knowledge. 19:3 [There is] no
speech nor language, [where] their voice is not heard. 19:4 Their line is gone
out through all the earth, and their words to the end of the world. In them
hath he set a tabernacle for the sun, 19:5 Which [is] as a bridegroom coming
out of his chamber, [and] rejoiceth as a strong man to run a race. 19:6 His

going forth [is] from the end of the heaven, and his circuit unto the ends of it: and there is nothing hid from the heat thereof. 19:7 The law of the LORD [is] perfect, converting the soul: the testimony of the LORD [is] sure, making wise the simple. 19:8 The statutes of the LORD [are] right, rejoicing the heart: the commandment of the LORD [is] pure, enlightening the eyes. 19:9 The fear of the LORD [is] clean, enduring for ever: the judgments of the LORD [are] true [and] righteous altogether. 19:10 More to be desired [are they] than gold, yea, than much fine gold: sweeter also than honey and the honeycomb. 19:11 Moreover by them is thy servant warned: [and] in keeping of them [there is] great reward. 19:12 Who can understand [his] errors? cleanse thou me from secret [faults]. 19:13 Keep back thy servant also from presumptuous [sins]; let them not have dominion over me: then shall I be upright, and I shall be innocent from the great transgression. 19:14 Let the words of my mouth, and the meditation of my heart, be acceptable in thy sight, O LORD, my strength, and my redeemer.

PSALM 20

To the chief Musician, A PSALM of David. 20:1 The LORD hear thee in the day of trouble; the name of the God of Jacob defend thee; 20:2 Send thee help from the sanctuary, and strengthen thee out of Zion; 20:3 Remember all thy offerings, and accept thy burnt sacrifice; Selah. 20:4 Grant thee according to thine own heart, and fulfil all thy counsel. 20:5 We will rejoice in thy salvation, and in the name of our God we will set up [our] banners: the LORD fulfil all thy petitions. 20:6 Now know I that the LORD saveth his anointed; he will hear him from his holy heaven with the saving strength of his right hand. 20:7 Some [trust] in chariots, and some in horses: but we will remember the name of the LORD our God. 20:8 They are brought down and fallen: but we are risen, and stand upright. 20:9 Save, LORD: let the king hear us when we call.

PSALM 21

To the chief Musician, A PSALM of David. 21:1 The king shall joy in thy strength, O LORD; and in thy salvation how greatly shall he rejoice! 21:2 Thou hast given him his heart's desire, and hast not withholden the request of his lips. Selah. 21:3 For thou preventest him with the blessings of goodness: thou settest a crown of pure gold on his head. 21:4 He asked life of thee, [and] thou gavest [it] him, [even] length of days for ever and ever. 21:5 His glory [is] great in thy salvation: honour and majesty hast thou laid upon him. 21:6 For thou hast made him most blessed for ever: thou hast made him exceeding glad with thy countenance. 21:7 For the king trusteth in the LORD, and through the mercy of the most High he shall not be moved. 21:8 Thine hand shall find out all thine enemies: thy right hand shall find out those that hate thee. 21:9 Thou shalt make them as a fiery oven in the time of thine anger: the LORD shall swallow them up in his wrath, and the fire shall devour them. 21:10 Their fruit shalt thou destroy from the earth, and their seed from among the children of men. 21:11 For they intended evil against thee: they imagined a mischievous device, [which] they are not able [to perform]. 21:12 Therefore shalt thou make them turn their back, [when] thou shalt make ready [thine arrows] upon thy strings against the face of them. 21:13 Be thou exalted, LORD, in thine own strength: [so] will we sing and praise thy power.

PSALM 22

To the chief Musician upon Aijeleth Shahar, A PSALM of David. 22:1 My God, my God, why hast thou forsaken me? [why art thou so] far from helping me, [and from] the words of my roaring? 22:2 O my God, I cry in the daytime, but thou hearest not; and in the night season, and am not silent. 22:3 But thou [art] holy, [O thou] that inhabitest the praises of Israel. 22:4 Our fathers trusted in thee: they trusted, and thou didst deliver them. 22:5 They cried unto thee, and were delivered: they trusted in thee, and were not confounded. 22:6 But I [am] a worm, and no man; a reproach of men, and despised of the people. 22:7 All they that see me laugh me to scorn: they shoot out the lip, they shake the head, [saying], 22:8 He trusted on the LORD [that] he would deliver him: let him deliver him, seeing he delighted

in him. 22:9 But thou [art] he that took me out of the womb: thou didst
make me hope [when I was] upon my mother's breasts. 22:10 I was cast upon
thee from the womb: thou [art] my God from my mother's belly. 22:11 Be
not far from me; for trouble [is] near; for [there is] none to help. 22:12 Many
bulls have compassed me: strong [bulls] of Bashan have beset me round.
22:13 They gaped upon me [with] their mouths, [as] a ravening and a roaring
lion. 22:14 I am poured out like water, and all my bones are out of joint: my
heart is like wax; it is melted in the midst of my bowels. 22:15 My strength
is dried up like a potsherd; and my tongue cleaveth to my jaws; and thou hast
brought me into the dust of death. 22:16 For dogs have compassed me: the
assembly of the wicked have inclosed me: they pierced my hands and my feet.
22:17 I may tell all my bones: they look [and] stare upon me. 22:18 They part
my garments among them, and cast lots upon my vesture. 22:19 But be not
thou far from me, O LORD: O my strength, haste thee to help me. 22:20
Deliver my soul from the sword; my darling from the power of the dog. 22:21
Save me from the lion's mouth: for thou hast heard me from the horns of the
unicorns. 22:22 I will declare thy name unto my brethren: in the midst of the
congregation will I praise thee. 22:23 Ye that fear the LORD, praise him; all
ye the seed of Jacob, glorify him; and fear him, all ye the seed of Israel. 22:24
For he hath not despised nor abhorred the affliction of the afflicted; neither
hath he hid his face from him; but when he cried unto him, he heard. 22:25
My praise [shall be] of thee in the great congregation: I will pay my vows
before them that fear him. 22:26 The meek shall eat and be satisfied: they
shall praise the LORD that seek him: your heart shall live for ever. 22:27 All
the ends of the world shall remember and turn unto the LORD: and all the
kindreds of the nations shall worship before thee. 22:28 For the kingdom [is]
the LORD's: and he [is] the governor among the nations. 22:29 All [they that
be] fat upon earth shall eat and worship: all they that go down to the dust
shall bow before him: and none can keep alive his own soul. 22:30 A seed
shall serve him; it shall be accounted to the Lord for a generation. 22:31
They shall come, and shall declare his righteousness unto a people that shall
be born, that he hath done [this].

PSALM 23

A PSALM of David. 23:1 The LORD [is] my shepherd; I shall not want. 23:2 He maketh me to lie down in green pastures: he leadeth me beside the still waters. 23:3 He restoreth my soul: he leadeth me in the paths of righteousness for his name's sake. 23:4 Yea, though I walk through the valley of the shadow of death, I will fear no evil: for thou [art] with me; thy rod and thy staff they comfort me. 23:5 Thou preparest a table before me in the presence of mine enemies: thou anointest my head with oil; my cup runneth over. 23:6 Surely goodness and mercy shall follow me all the days of my life: and I will dwell in the house of the LORD for ever.

PSALM 24

A PSALM of David. 24:1 The earth [is] the LORD's, and the fulness thereof; the world, and they that dwell therein. 24:2 For he hath founded it upon the seas, and established it upon the floods. 24:3 Who shall ascend into the hill of the LORD? or who shall stand in his holy place? 24:4 He that hath clean hands, and a pure heart; who hath not lifted up his soul unto vanity, nor sworn deceitfully. 24:5 He shall receive the blessing from the LORD, and righteousness from the God of his salvation. 24:6 This [is] the generation of them that seek him, that seek thy face, O Jacob. Selah. 24:7 Lift up your heads, O ye gates; and be ye lift up, ye everlasting doors; and the King of glory shall come in. 24:8 Who [is] this King of glory? The LORD strong and mighty, the LORD mighty in battle. 24:9 Lift up your heads, O ye gates; even lift [them] up, ye everlasting doors; and the King of glory shall come in. 24:10 Who is this King of glory? The LORD of hosts, he [is] the King of glory. Selah.

PSALM 25

[A PSALM] of David. 25:1 Unto thee, O LORD, do I lift up my soul. 25:2 O my God, I trust in thee: let me not be ashamed, let not mine enemies triumph over me. 25:3 Yea, let none that wait on thee be ashamed: let them be ashamed which transgress without cause. 25:4 Shew me thy ways, O

LORD; teach me thy paths. 25:5 Lead me in thy truth, and teach me: for thou [art] the God of my salvation; on thee do I wait all the day. 25:6 Remember, O LORD, thy tender mercies and thy lovingkindnesses; for they [have been] ever of old. 25:7 Remember not the sins of my youth, nor my transgressions: according to thy mercy remember thou me for thy goodness' sake, O LORD. 25:8 Good and upright [is] the LORD: therefore will he teach sinners in the way. 25:9 The meek will he guide in judgment: and the meek will he teach his way. 25:10 All the paths of the LORD [are] mercy and truth unto such as keep his covenant and his testimonies. 25:11 For thy name's sake, O LORD, pardon mine iniquity; for it [is] great. 25:12 What man [is] he that feareth the LORD? him shall he teach in the way [that] he shall choose. 25:13 His soul shall dwell at ease; and his seed shall inherit the earth. 25:14 The secret of the LORD [is] with them that fear him; and he will shew them his covenant. 25:15 Mine eyes [are] ever toward the LORD; for he shall pluck my feet out of the net. 25:16 Turn thee unto me, and have mercy upon me; for I [am] desolate and afflicted. 25:17 The troubles of my heart are enlarged: [O] bring thou me out of my distresses. 25:18 Look upon mine affliction and my pain; and forgive all my sins. 25:19 Consider mine enemies; for they are many; and they hate me with cruel hatred. 25:20 O keep my soul, and deliver me: let me not be ashamed; for I put my trust in thee. 25:21 Let integrity and uprightness preserve me; for I wait on thee. 25:22 Redeem Israel, O God, out of all his troubles.

PSALM 26

[A PSALM] of David. 26:1 Judge me, O LORD; for I have walked in mine integrity: I have trusted also in the LORD; [therefore] I shall not slide. 26:2 Examine me, O LORD, and prove me; try my reins and my heart. 26:3 For thy lovingkindness [is] before mine eyes: and I have walked in thy truth. 26:4 I have not sat with vain persons, neither will I go in with dissemblers. 26:5 I have hated the congregation of evil doers; and will not sit with the wicked. 26:6 I will wash mine hands in innocency: so will I compass thine altar, O LORD: 26:7 That I may publish with the voice of thanksgiving, and tell of all thy wondrous works. 26:8 LORD, I have loved the habitation of thy house, and the place where thine honour dwelleth. 26:9 Gather not my soul with sinners, nor my life with bloody men: 26:10 In whose hands [is] mischief, and their right hand is full of bribes. 26:11 But as for me, I will walk in mine integrity: redeem me, and be merciful unto me. 26:12 My foot standeth in an even place: in the congregations will I bless the LORD.

PSALM 27

[A PSALM] of David. 27:1 The LORD [is] my light and my salvation; whom shall I fear? the LORD [is] the strength of my life; of whom shall I be afraid? 27:2 When the wicked, [even] mine enemies and my foes, came upon me to eat up my flesh, they stumbled and fell. 27:3 Though an host should encamp against me, my heart shall not fear: though war should rise against me, in this [will] I [be] confident. 27:4 One [thing] have I desired of the LORD, that will I seek after; that I may dwell in the house of the LORD all the days of my life, to behold the beauty of the LORD, and to inquire in his temple. 27:5 For in the time of trouble he shall hide me in his pavilion: in the secret of his tabernacle shall he hide me; he shall set me up upon a rock. 27:6 And now shall mine head be lifted up above mine enemies round about me: therefore will I offer in his tabernacle sacrifices of joy; I will sing, yea, I will sing praises unto the LORD. 27:7 Hear, O LORD, [when] I cry with my voice: have mercy also upon me, and answer me. 27:8 [When thou saidst], Seek ye my face; my heart said unto thee, Thy face, LORD, will I seek. 27:9 Hide not thy face [far] from me; put not thy servant away in anger: thou hast been my help; leave me not, neither forsake me, O God of my salvation. 27:10 When my father and my mother forsake me, then the LORD will take me up. 27:11 Teach me thy way, O LORD, and lead me in a plain path, because of mine enemies. 27:12 Deliver me not over unto the will of mine enemies: for false witnesses are risen up against me, and such as breathe out cruelty. 27:13 [I had fainted], unless I had believed to see the goodness of the LORD in the land of the living. 27:14 Wait on the LORD: be of good courage, and he shall strengthen thine heart: wait, I say, on the LORD.

PSALMS

PSALM 28

[A PSALM] of David. 28:1 Unto thee will I cry, O LORD my rock; be not silent to me: lest, [if] thou be silent to me, I become like them that go down into the pit. 28:2 Hear the voice of my supplications, when I cry unto thee, when I lift up my hands toward thy holy oracle. 28:3 Draw me not away with the wicked, and with the workers of iniquity, which speak peace to their neighbours, but mischief [is] in their hearts. 28:4 Give them according to their deeds, and according to the wickedness of their endeavours: give them after the work of their hands; render to them their desert. 28:5 Because they regard not the works of the LORD, nor the operation of his hands, he shall destroy them, and not build them up. 28:6 Blessed [be] the LORD, because he hath heard the voice of my supplications. 28:7 The LORD [is] my strength and my shield; my heart trusted in him, and I am helped: therefore my heart greatly rejoiceth; and with my song will I praise him. 28:8 The LORD [is] their strength, and he [is] the saving strength of his anointed. 28:9 Save thy people, and bless thine inheritance: feed them also, and lift them up for ever.

PSALM 29

A PSALM of David. 29:1 Give unto the LORD, O ye mighty, give unto the LORD glory and strength. 29:2 Give unto the LORD the glory due unto his name; worship the LORD in the beauty of holiness. 29:3 The voice of the LORD [is] upon the waters: the God of glory thundereth: the LORD [is] upon many waters. 29:4 The voice of the LORD [is] powerful; the voice of the LORD [is] full of majesty. 29:5 The voice of the LORD breaketh the cedars; yea, the LORD breaketh the cedars of Lebanon. 29:6 He maketh them also to skip like a calf; Lebanon and Sirion like a young unicorn. 29:7 The voice of the LORD divideth the flames of fire. 29:8 The voice of the LORD shaketh the wilderness; the LORD shaketh the wilderness of Kadesh. 29:9 The voice of the LORD maketh the hinds to calve, and discovereth the forests: and in his temple doth every one speak of [his] glory. 29:10 The LORD sitteth upon the flood; yea, the LORD sitteth King for ever. 29:11 The LORD will give strength unto his people; the LORD will bless his people with peace.

PSALM 30

A PSALM [and] Song [at] the dedication of the house of David. 30:1 I will extol thee, O LORD; for thou hast lifted me up, and hast not made my foes to rejoice over me. 30:2 O LORD my God, I cried unto thee, and thou hast healed me. 30:3 O LORD, thou hast brought up my soul from the grave: thou hast kept me alive, that I should not go down to the pit. 30:4 Sing unto the LORD, O ye saints of his, and give thanks at the remembrance of his holiness. 30:5 For his anger [endureth but] a moment; in his favour [is] life: weeping may endure for a night, but joy [cometh] in the morning. 30:6 And in my prosperity I said, I shall never be moved. 30:7 LORD, by thy favour thou hast made my mountain to stand strong: thou didst hide thy face, [and] I was troubled. 30:8 I cried to thee, O LORD; and unto the LORD I made supplication. 30:9 What profit [is there] in my blood, when I go down to the pit? Shall the dust praise thee? shall it declare thy truth? 30:10 Hear, O LORD, and have mercy upon me: LORD, be thou my helper. 30:11 Thou hast turned for me my mourning into dancing: thou hast put off my sackcloth, and girded me with gladness; 30:12 To the end that [my] glory may sing praise to thee, and not be silent. O LORD my God, I will give thanks unto thee for ever.

PSALM 31

To the chief Musician, A PSALM of David. 31:1 In thee, O LORD, do I put my trust; let me never be ashamed: deliver me in thy righteousness. 31:2 Bow down thine ear to me; deliver me speedily: be thou my strong rock, for an house of defence to save me. 31:3 For thou [art] my rock and my fortress; therefore for thy name's sake lead me, and guide me. 31:4 Pull me out of the net that they have laid privily for me: for thou [art] my strength. 31:5 Into thine hand I commit my spirit: thou hast redeemed me, O LORD God of truth. 31:6 I have hated them that regard lying vanities: but I trust in the LORD. 31:7 I will be glad and rejoice in thy mercy: for thou hast considered my trouble; thou hast known my soul in adversities; 31:8 And hast not shut me up into the hand of the enemy: thou hast set my feet in a large room. 31:9 Have mercy upon me, O LORD, for I am in trouble: mine eye is consumed with grief, [yea], my soul and my belly. 31:10 For my life is spent with grief, and my years with sighing: my strength faileth because of mine iniquity, and my bones are consumed. 31:11 I was a reproach among all mine enemies, but especially among my neighbours, and a fear to mine acquaintance: they that did see me without fled from me. 31:12 I am forgotten as a dead man out of mind: I am like a broken vessel. 31:13 For I have heard the slander of many: fear [was] on every side: while they took counsel together against me, they devised to take away my life. 31:14 But I trusted in thee, O LORD: I said, Thou [art] my God. 31:15 My times [are] in thy hand: deliver me from the hand of mine enemies, and from them that persecute me. 31:16 Make thy face to shine upon thy servant: save me for thy mercies' sake. 31:17 Let me not be ashamed, O LORD; for I have called upon thee: let the wicked be ashamed, [and] let them be silent in the grave. 31:18 Let the lying libe put to silence; which speak grievous things proudly and contemptuously against the righteous. 31:19 [Oh] how great [is] thy goodness, which thou hast laid up for them that fear thee; [which] thou hast wrought for them that trust in thee before the sons of men! 31:20 Thou shalt hide them in the secret of thy presence from the pride of man: thou shalt keep them secretly in a pavilion from the strife of tongues. 31:21 Blessed [be] the LORD: for he hath shewed me his marvellous kindness in a strong city. 31:22 For I said in my haste, I am cut off from before thine eyes: nevertheless thou heardest the voice of my supplications when I cried unto thee. 31:23 O love the LORD, all ye his saints: [for] the LORD preserveth the faithful, and plentifully rewardeth the proud doer. 31:24 Be of good courage, and he shall strengthen your heart, all ye that hope in the LORD.

PSALM 32

[A PSALM] of David, Maschil. 32:1 Blessed [is he whose] transgression [is] forgiven, [whose] sin [is] covered. 32:2 Blessed [is] the man unto whom the

LORD imputeth not iniquity, and in whose spirit [there is] no guile. 32:3 When I kept silence, my bones waxed old through my roaring all the day long. 32:4 For day and night thy hand was heavy upon me: my moisture is turned into the drought of summer. Selah. 32:5 I acknowledged my sin unto thee, and mine iniquity have I not hid. I said, I will confess my transgressions unto the LORD; and thou forgavest the iniquity of my sin. Selah. 32:6 For this shall every one that is godly pray unto thee in a time when thou mayest be found: surely in the floods of great waters they shall not come nigh unto him. 32:7 Thou [art] my hiding place; thou shalt preserve me from trouble; thou shalt compass me about with songs of deliverance. Selah. 32:8 I will instruct thee and teach thee in the way which thou shalt go: I will guide thee with mine eye. 32:9 Be ye not as the horse, [or] as the mule, [which] have no understanding: whose mouth must be held in with bit and bridle, lest they come near unto thee. 32:10 Many sorrows [shall be] to the wicked: but he that trusteth in the LORD, mercy shall compass him about. 32:11 Be glad in the LORD, and rejoice, ye righteous: and shout for joy, all [ye that are] upright in heart.

PSALM 33

33:1 Rejoice in the LORD, O ye righteous: [for] praise is comely for the upright. 33:2 Praise the LORD with harp: sing unto him with the psaltery [and] an instrument of ten strings. 33:3 Sing unto him a new song; play skilfully with a loud noise. 33:4 For the word of the LORD [is] right; and all his works [are done] in truth. 33:5 He loveth righteousness and judgment: the earth is full of the goodness of the LORD. 33:6 By the word of the LORD were the heavens made; and all the host of them by the breath of his mouth. 33:7 He gathereth the waters of the sea together as an heap: he layeth up the depth in storehouses. 33:8 Let all the earth fear the LORD: let all the inhabitants of the world stand in awe of him. 33:9 For he spake, and it was [done]; he commanded, and it stood fast. 33:10 The LORD bringeth the counsel of the heathen to nought: he maketh the devices of the people of none effect. 33:11 The counsel of the LORD standeth for ever, the thoughts of his heart to all generations. 33:12 Blessed [is] the nation whose God [is] the LORD; [and] the people [whom] he hath chosen for his own inheritance. 33:13 The LORD looketh from heaven; he beholdeth all the sons of men. 33:14 From the place of his habitation he looketh upon all the inhabitants of the earth. 33:15 He fashioneth their hearts alike; he considereth all their works. 33:16 There is no king saved by the multitude of an host: a mighty man is not delivered by much strength. 33:17 An horse [is] a vain thing for safety: neither shall he deliver [any] by his great strength. 33:18 Behold, the eye of the LORD [is] upon them that fear him, upon them that hope in his mercy; 33:19 To deliver their soul from death, and to keep them alive in famine. 33:20 Our soul waiteth for the LORD: he [is] our help and our shield. 33:21 For our heart shall rejoice in him, because we have trusted in his holy name. 33:22 Let thy mercy, O LORD, be upon us, according as we hope in thee.

PSALM 34
[A PSALM] of David, when he changed his behaviour before Abimelech; who drove him away, and he departed. 34:1 I will bless the LORD at all times: his praise [shall] continually [be] in my mouth. 34:2 My soul shall make her boast in the LORD: the humble shall hear [thereof], and be glad. 34:3 O magnify the LORD with me, and let us exalt his name together. 34:4 I sought the LORD, and he heard me, and delivered me from all my fears. 34:5 They looked unto him, and were lightened: and their faces were not ashamed. 34:6 This poor man cried, and the LORD heard [him], and saved him out of all his troubles. 34:7 The angel of the LORD encampeth round about them that fear him, and delivereth them. 34:8 O taste and see that the LORD [is] good: blessed [is] the man [that] trusteth in him. 34:9 O fear the LORD, ye his saints: for [there is] no want to them that fear him. 34:10 The young lions do lack, and suffer hunger: but they that seek the LORD shall not want any good [thing]. 34:11 Come, ye children, hearken unto me: I will teach you the fear of the LORD. 34:12 What man [is he that] desireth life, [and] loveth [many] days, that he may see good? 34:13 Keep thy tongue from evil, and thy

lifrom speaking guile. 34:14 Depart from evil, and do good; seek peace, and pursue it. 34:15 The eyes of the LORD [are] upon the righteous, and his ears [are open] unto their cry. 34:16 The face of the LORD [is] against them that do evil, to cut off the remembrance of them from the earth. 34:17 [The righteous] cry, and the LORD heareth, and delivereth them out of all their troubles. 34:18 The LORD [is] nigh unto them that are of a broken heart; and saveth such as be of a contrite spirit. 34:19 Many [are] the afflictions of the righteous: but the LORD delivereth him out of them all. 34:20 He keepeth all his bones: not one of them is broken. 34:21 Evil shall slay the wicked: and they that hate the righteous shall be desolate. 34:22 The LORD redeemeth the soul of his servants: and none of them that trust in him shall be desolate.

PSALM 35

[A PSALM] of David. 35:1 Plead [my cause], O LORD, with them that strive with me: fight against them that fight against me. 35:2 Take hold of shield and buckler, and stand up for mine help. 35:3 Draw out also the spear, and stop [the way] against them that persecute me: say unto my soul, I [am] thy salvation. 35:4 Let them be confounded and put to shame that seek after my soul: let them be turned back and brought to confusion that devise my hurt. 35:5 Let them be as chaff before the wind: and let the angel of the LORD chase [them]. 35:6 Let their way be dark and slippery: and let the angel of the LORD persecute them. 35:7 For without cause have they hid for me their net [in] a pit, [which] without cause they have digged for my soul. 35:8 Let destruction come upon him at unawares; and let his net that he hath hid catch himself: into that very destruction let him fall. 35:9 And my soul shall be joyful in the LORD: it shall rejoice in his salvation. 35:10 All my bones shall say, LORD, who [is] like unto thee, which deliverest the poor from him that is too strong for him, yea, the poor and the needy from him that spoileth him? 35:11 False witnesses did rise up; they laid to my charge [things] that I knew not. 35:12 They rewarded me evil for good [to] the spoiling of my soul. 35:13 But as for me, when they were sick, my clothing [was] sackcloth: I

humbled my soul with fasting; and my prayer returned into mine own
bosom. 35:14 I behaved myself as though [he had been] my friend [or]
brother: I bowed down heavily, as one that mourneth [for his] mother. 35:15
But in mine adversity they rejoiced, and gathered themselves together: [yea],
the abjects gathered themselves together against me, and I knew [it] not; they
did tear [me], and ceased not: 35:16 With hypocritical mockers in feasts, they
gnashed upon me with their teeth. 35:17 Lord, how long wilt thou look on?
rescue my soul from their destructions, my darling from the lions. 35:18 I
will give thee thanks in the great congregation: I will praise thee among much
people. 35:19 Let not them that are mine enemies wrongfully rejoice over
me: [neither] let them wink with the eye that hate me without a cause. 35:20
For they speak not peace: but they devise deceitful matters against [them that
are] quiet in the land. 35:21 Yea, they opened their mouth wide against me,
[and] said, Aha, aha, our eye hath seen [it]. 35:22 [This] thou hast seen, O
LORD: keep not silence: O Lord, be not far from me. 35:23 Stir up thyself,
and awake to my judgment, [even] unto my cause, my God and my Lord.
35:24 Judge me, O LORD my God, according to thy righteousness; and let
them not rejoice over me. 35:25 Let them not say in their hearts, Ah, so
would we have it: let them not say, We have swallowed him up. 35:26 Let
them be ashamed and brought to confusion together that rejoice at mine
hurt: let them be clothed with shame and dishonour that magnify
[themselves] against me. 35:27 Let them shout for joy, and be glad, that
favour my righteous cause: yea, let them say continually, Let the LORD be
magnified, which hath pleasure in the prosperity of his servant. 35:28 And
my tongue shall speak of thy righteousness [and] of thy praise all the day long.

PSALM 36

To the chief Musician, [A PSALM] of David the servant of the LORD. 36:1
The transgression of the wicked saith within my heart, [that there is] no fear
of God before his eyes. 36:2 For he flattereth himself in his own eyes, until
his iniquity be found to be hateful. 36:3 The words of his mouth [are]
iniquity and deceit: he hath left off to be wise, [and] to do good. 36:4 He

deviseth mischief upon his bed; he setteth himself in a way [that is] not good;
he abhorreth not evil. 36:5 Thy mercy, O LORD, [is] in the heavens; [and]
thy faithfulness [reacheth] unto the clouds. 36:6 Thy righteousness [is] like
the great mountains; thy judgments [are] a great deep: O LORD, thou
preservest man and beast. 36:7 How excellent [is] thy lovingkindness, O God!
therefore the children of men put their trust under the shadow of thy wings.
36:8 They shall be abundantly satisfied with the fatness of thy house; and
thou shalt make them drink of the river of thy pleasures. 36:9 For with thee
[is] the fountain of life: in thy light shall we see light. 36:10 O continue thy
lovingkindness unto them that know thee; and thy righteousness to the
upright in heart. 36:11 Let not the foot of pride come against me, and let not
the hand of the wicked remove me. 36:12 There are the workers of iniquity
fallen: they are cast down, and shall not be able to rise.

PSALM 37

[A PSALM] of David. 37:1 Fret not thyself because of evildoers, neither be
thou envious against the workers of iniquity. 37:2 For they shall soon be cut
down like the grass, and wither as the green herb. 37:3 Trust in the LORD,
and do good; [so] shalt thou dwell in the land, and verily thou shalt be fed.
37:4 Delight thyself also in the LORD; and he shall give thee the desires of
thine heart. 37:5 Commit thy way unto the LORD; trust also in him; and he
shall bring [it] to pass. 37:6 And he shall bring forth thy righteousness as the
light, and thy judgment as the noonday. 37:7 Rest in the LORD, and wait
patiently for him: fret not thyself because of him who prospereth in his way,
because of the man who bringeth wicked devices to pass. 37:8 Cease from
anger, and forsake wrath: fret not thyself in any wise to do evil. 37:9 For
evildoers shall be cut off: but those that wait upon the LORD, they shall
inherit the earth. 37:10 For yet a little while, and the wicked [shall] not [be]:
yea, thou shalt diligently consider his place, and it [shall] not [be]. 37:11 But
the meek shall inherit the earth; and shall delight themselves in the
abundance of peace. 37:12 The wicked plotteth against the just, and gnasheth
upon him with his teeth. 37:13 The Lord shall laugh at him: for he seeth that

his day is coming. 37:14 The wicked have drawn out the sword, and have bent their bow, to cast down the poor and needy, [and] to slay such as be of upright conversation. 37:15 Their sword shall enter into their own heart, and their bows shall be broken. 37:16 A little that a righteous man hath [is] better than the riches of many wicked. 37:17 For the arms of the wicked shall be broken: but the LORD upholdeth the righteous. 37:18 The LORD knoweth the days of the upright: and their inheritance shall be for ever. 37:19 They shall not be ashamed in the evil time: and in the days of famine they shall be satisfied. 37:20 But the wicked shall perish, and the enemies of the LORD [shall be] as the fat of lambs: they shall consume; into smoke shall they consume away. 37:21 The wicked borroweth, and payeth not again: but the righteous sheweth mercy, and giveth. 37:22 For [such as be] blessed of him shall inherit the earth; and [they that be] cursed of him shall be cut off. 37:23 The steof a [good] man are ordered by the LORD: and he delighteth in his way. 37:24 Though he fall, he shall not be utterly cast down: for the LORD upholdeth [him with] his hand. 37:25 I have been young, and [now] am old; yet have I not seen the righteous forsaken, nor his seed begging bread. 37:26 [He is] ever merciful, and lendeth; and his seed [is] blessed. 37:27 Depart from evil, and do good; and dwell for evermore. 37:28 For the LORD loveth judgment, and forsaketh not his saints; they are preserved for ever: but the seed of the wicked shall be cut off. 37:29 The righteous shall inherit the land, and dwell therein for ever. 37:30 The mouth of the righteous speaketh wisdom, and his tongue talketh of judgment. 37:31 The law of his God [is] in his heart; none of his steshall slide. 37:32 The wicked watcheth the righteous, and seeketh to slay him. 37:33 The LORD will not leave him in his hand, nor condemn him when he is judged. 37:34 Wait on the LORD, and keep his way, and he shall exalt thee to inherit the land: when the wicked are cut off, thou shalt see [it]. 37:35 I have seen the wicked in great power, and spreading himself like a green bay tree. 37:36 Yet he passed away, and, lo, he [was] not: yea, I sought him, but he could not be found. 37:37 Mark the perfect [man], and behold the upright: for the end of [that] man [is] peace. 37:38 But the transgressors shall be destroyed together: the end of the wicked shall be cut off. 37:39 But the salvation of the righteous [is] of the LORD: [he is] their strength in the time of trouble. 37:40 And the LORD shall help them, and deliver them: he shall deliver them from the wicked, and save them, because they trust in him.

PSALM 38

A PSALM of David, to bring to remembrance. 38:1 O LORD, rebuke me not in thy wrath: neither chasten me in thy hot displeasure. 38:2 For thine arrows stick fast in me, and thy hand presseth me sore. 38:3 [There is] no soundness in my flesh because of thine anger; neither [is there any] rest in my bones because of my sin. 38:4 For mine iniquities are gone over mine head: as an heavy burden they are too heavy for me. 38:5 My wounds stink [and] are corrupt because of my foolishness. 38:6 I am troubled; I am bowed down greatly; I go mourning all the day long. 38:7 For my loins are filled with a loathsome [disease]: and [there is] no soundness in my flesh. 38:8 I am feeble and sore broken: I have roared by reason of the disquietness of my heart. 38:9 Lord, all my desire [is] before thee; and my groaning is not hid from thee. 38:10 My heart panteth, my strength faileth me: as for the light of mine eyes, it also is gone from me. 38:11 My lovers and my friends stand aloof from my sore; and my kinsmen stand afar off. 38:12 They also that seek after my life lay snares [for me]: and they that seek my hurt speak mischievous things, and imagine deceits all the day long. 38:13 But I, as a deaf [man], heard not; and [I was] as a dumb man [that] openeth not his mouth. 38:14 Thus I was as a man that heareth not, and in whose mouth [are] no reproofs. 38:15 For in thee, O LORD, do I hope: thou wilt hear, O Lord my God. 38:16 For I said, [Hear me], lest [otherwise] they should rejoice over me: when my foot slippeth, they magnify [themselves] against me. 38:17 For I [am] ready to halt, and my sorrow [is] continually before me. 38:18 For I will declare mine iniquity; I will be sorry for my sin. 38:19 But mine enemies [are] lively, [and] they are strong: and they that hate me wrongfully are multiplied. 38:20 They also that render evil for good are mine adversaries; because I follow [the thing that] good [is]. 38:21 Forsake me not, O LORD: O my God, be not far from me. 38:22 Make haste to help me, O Lord my salvation.

PSALM 39

To the chief Musician, [even] to Jeduthun, A PSALM of David. 39:1 I said, I will take heed to my ways, that I sin not with my tongue: I will keep my mouth with a bridle, while the wicked is before me. 39:2 I was dumb with silence, I held my peace, [even] from good; and my sorrow was stirred. 39:3 My heart was hot within me, while I was musing the fire burned: [then] spake I with my tongue, 39:4 LORD, make me to know mine end, and the measure of my days, what it [is; that] I may know how frail I [am]. 39:5 Behold, thou hast made my days [as] an handbreadth; and mine age [is] as nothing before thee: verily every man at his best state [is] altogether vanity. Selah. 39:6 Surely every man walketh in a vain shew: surely they are disquieted in vain: he heapeth up [riches], and knoweth not who shall gather them. 39:7 And now, Lord, what wait I for? my hope [is] in thee. 39:8 Deliver me from all my transgressions: make me not the reproach of the foolish. 39:9 I was dumb, I opened not my mouth; because thou didst [it]. 39:10 Remove thy stroke away from me: I am consumed by the blow of thine hand. 39:11 When thou with rebukes dost correct man for iniquity, thou makest his beauty to consume away like a moth: surely every man [is] vanity. Selah. 39:12 Hear my prayer, O LORD, and give ear unto my cry; hold not thy peace at my tears: for I [am] a stranger with thee, [and] a sojourner, as all my fathers [were]. 39:13 O spare me, that I may recover strength, before I go hence, and be no more.

PSALM 40

To the chief Musician, A PSALM of David. 40:1 I waited patiently for the LORD; and he inclined unto me, and heard my cry. 40:2 He brought me up also out of an horrible pit, out of the miry clay, and set my feet upon a rock, [and] established my goings. 40:3 And he hath put a new song in my mouth, [even] praise unto our God: many shall see [it], and fear, and shall trust in the LORD. 40:4 Blessed [is] that man that maketh the LORD his trust, and respecteth not the proud, nor such as turn aside to lies. 40:5 Many, O LORD

my God, [are] thy wonderful works [which] thou hast done, and thy thoughts [which are] to us-ward: they cannot be reckoned up in order unto thee: [if] I would declare and speak [of them], they are more than can be numbered.
40:6 Sacrifice and offering thou didst not desire; mine ears hast thou opened: burnt offering and sin offering hast thou not required. 40:7 Then said I, Lo, I come: in the volume of the book [it is] written of me, 40:8 I delight to do thy will, O my God: yea, thy law [is] within my heart. 40:9 I have preached righteousness in the great congregation: lo, I have not refrained my lips, O LORD, thou knowest. 40:10 I have not hid thy righteousness within my heart; I have declared thy faithfulness and thy salvation: I have not concealed thy lovingkindness and thy truth from the great congregation. 40:11 Withhold not thou thy tender mercies from me, O LORD: let thy lovingkindness and thy truth continually preserve me. 40:12 For innumerable evils have compassed me about: mine iniquities have taken hold upon me, so that I am not able to look up; they are more than the hairs of mine head: therefore my heart faileth me. 40:13 Be pleased, O LORD, to deliver me: O LORD, make haste to help me. 40:14 Let them be ashamed and confounded together that seek after my soul to destroy it; let them be driven backward and put to shame that wish me evil. 40:15 Let them be desolate for a reward of their shame that say unto me, Aha, aha. 40:16 Let all those that seek thee rejoice and be glad in thee: let such as love thy salvation say continually, The LORD be magnified. 40:17 But I [am] poor and needy; [yet] the Lord thinketh upon me: thou [art] my help and my deliverer; make no tarrying, O my God.

PSALM 41

To the chief Musician, A PSALM of David. 41:1 Blessed [is] he that considereth the poor: the LORD will deliver him in time of trouble. 41:2 The LORD will preserve him, and keep him alive; [and] he shall be blessed upon the earth: and thou wilt not deliver him unto the will of his enemies.
41:3 The LORD will strengthen him upon the bed of languishing: thou wilt make all his bed in his sickness. 41:4 I said, LORD, be merciful unto me:

heal my soul; for I have sinned against thee. 41:5 Mine enemies speak evil of
me, When shall he die, and his name perish? 41:6 And if he come to see
[me], he speaketh vanity: his heart gathereth iniquity to itself; [when] he
goeth abroad, he telleth [it]. 41:7 All that hate me whisper together against
me: against me do they devise my hurt. 41:8 An evil disease, [say they],
cleaveth fast unto him: and [now] that he lieth he shall rise up no more. 41:9
Yea, mine own familiar friend, in whom I trusted, which did eat of my bread,
hath lifted up [his] heel against me. 41:10 But thou, O LORD, be merciful
unto me, and raise me up, that I may requite them. 41:11 By this I know that
thou favourest me, because mine enemy doth not triumph over me. 41:12
And as for me, thou upholdest me in mine integrity, and settest me before
thy face for ever. 41:13 Blessed [be] the LORD God of Israel from everlasting,
and to everlasting. Amen, and Amen.

PSALM 42

To the chief Musician, Maschil, for the sons of Korah. 42:1 As the hart
panteth after the water brooks, so panteth my soul after thee, O God. 42:2
My soul thirsteth for God, for the living God: when shall I come and appear
before God? 42:3 My tears have been my meat day and night, while they
continually say unto me, Where [is] thy God? 42:4 When I remember these
[things], I pour out my soul in me: for I had gone with the multitude, I went
with them to the house of God, with the voice of joy and praise, with a
multitude that kept holyday. 42:5 Why art thou cast down, O my soul? and
[why] art thou disquieted in me? hope thou in God: for I shall yet praise him
[for] the help of his countenance. 42:6 O my God, my soul is cast down
within me: therefore will I remember thee from the land of Jordan, and of
the Hermonites, from the hill Mizar. 42:7 Deep calleth unto deep at the
noise of thy waterspouts: all thy waves and thy billows are gone over me. 42:8
[Yet] the LORD will command his lovingkindness in the daytime, and in the
night his song [shall be] with me, [and] my prayer unto the God of my life.
42:9 I will say unto God my rock, Why hast thou forgotten me? why go I
mourning because of the oppression of the enemy? 42:10 [As] with a sword

in my bones, mine enemies reproach me; while they say daily unto me, Where [is] thy God? 42:11 Why art thou cast down, O my soul? and why art thou disquieted within me? hope thou in God: for I shall yet praise him, [who is] the health of my countenance, and my God.

PSALM 43

43:1 Judge me, O God, and plead my cause against an ungodly nation: O deliver me from the deceitful and unjust man. 43:2 For thou [art] the God of my strength: why dost thou cast me off? why go I mourning because of the oppression of the enemy? 43:3 O send out thy light and thy truth: let them lead me; let them bring me unto thy holy hill, and to thy tabernacles. 43:4 Then will I go unto the altar of God, unto God my exceeding joy: yea, upon the harp will I praise thee, O God my God. 43:5 Why art thou cast down, O my soul? and why art thou disquieted within me? hope in God: for I shall yet praise him, [who is] the health of my countenance, and my God.

PSALM 44

To the chief Musician for the sons of Korah, Maschil. 44:1 We have heard with our ears, O God, our fathers have told us, [what] work thou didst in their days, in the times of old. 44:2 [How] thou didst drive out the heathen with thy hand, and plantedst them; [how] thou didst afflict the people, and cast them out. 44:3 For they got not the land in possession by their own sword, neither did their own arm save them: but thy right hand, and thine arm, and the light of thy countenance, because thou hadst a favour unto them. 44:4 Thou art my King, O God: command deliverances for Jacob. 44:5 Through thee will we push down our enemies: through thy name will we tread them under that rise up against us. 44:6 For I will not trust in my bow, neither shall my sword save me. 44:7 But thou hast saved us from our enemies, and hast put them to shame that hated us. 44:8 In God we boast all the day long, and praise thy name for ever. Selah. 44:9 But thou hast cast off, and put us to shame; and goest not forth with our armies. 44:10 Thou makest us to turn back from the enemy: and they which hate us spoil for

themselves. 44:11 Thou hast given us like sheep [appointed] for meat; and
hast scattered us among the heathen. 44:12 Thou sellest thy people for
nought, and dost not increase [thy wealth] by their price. 44:13 Thou makest
us a reproach to our neighbours, a scorn and a derision to them that are
round about us. 44:14 Thou makest us a byword among the heathen, a
shaking of the head among the people. 44:15 My confusion [is] continually
before me, and the shame of my face hath covered me, 44:16 For the voice
of him that reproacheth and blasphemeth; by reason of the enemy and
avenger. 44:17 All this is come upon us; yet have we not forgotten thee,
neither have we dealt falsely in thy covenant. 44:18 Our heart is not turned
back, neither have our stedeclined from thy way; 44:19 Though thou hast
sore broken us in the place of dragons, and covered us with the shadow of
death. 44:20 If we have forgotten the name of our God, or stretched out our
hands to a strange god; 44:21 Shall not God search this out? for he knoweth
the secrets of the heart. 44:22 Yea, for thy sake are we killed all the day long;
we are counted as sheep for the slaughter. 44:23 Awake, why sleepest thou,
O Lord? arise, cast [us] not off for ever. 44:24 Wherefore hidest thou thy face,
[and] forgettest our affliction and our oppression? 44:25 For our soul is
bowed down to the dust: our belly cleaveth unto the earth. 44:26 Arise for
our help, and redeem us for thy mercies' sake.

PSALM 45

To the chief Musician upon Shoshannim, for the sons of Korah, Maschil, A
Song of loves. 45:1 My heart is inditing a good matter: I speak of the things
which I have made touching the king: my tongue [is] the pen of a ready
writer. 45:2 Thou art fairer than the children of men: grace is poured into
thy lips: therefore God hath blessed thee for ever. 45:3 Gird thy sword upon
[thy] thigh, O [most] mighty, with thy glory and thy majesty. 45:4 And in thy
majesty ride prosperously because of truth and meekness [and] righteousness;
and thy right hand shall teach thee terrible things. 45:5 Thine arrows [are]
sharp in the heart of the king's enemies; [whereby] the people fall under thee.
45:6 Thy throne, O God, [is] for ever and ever: the sceptre of thy kingdom

[is] a right sceptre. 45:7 Thou lovest righteousness, and hatest wickedness: therefore God, thy God, hath anointed thee with the oil of gladness above thy fellows. 45:8 All thy garments [smell] of myrrh, and aloes, [and] cassia, out of the ivory palaces, whereby they have made thee glad. 45:9 Kings' daughters [were] among thy honourable women: upon thy right hand did stand the queen in gold of Ophir. 45:10 Hearken, O daughter, and consider, and incline thine ear; forget also thine own people, and thy father's house; 45:11 So shall the king greatly desire thy beauty: for he [is] thy Lord; and worship thou him. 45:12 And the daughter of Tyre [shall be there] with a gift; [even] the rich among the people shall intreat thy favour. 45:13 The king's daughter [is] all glorious within: her clothing [is] of wrought gold. 45:14 She shall be brought unto the king in raiment of needlework: the virgins her companions that follow her shall be brought unto thee. 45:15 With gladness and rejoicing shall they be brought: they shall enter into the king's palace. 45:16 Instead of thy fathers shall be thy children, whom thou mayest make princes in all the earth. 45:17 I will make thy name to be remembered in all generations: therefore shall the people praise thee for ever and ever.

PSALM 46

To the chief Musician for the sons of Korah, A Song upon Alamoth. 46:1 God [is] our refuge and strength, a very present help in trouble. 46:2 Therefore will not we fear, though the earth be removed, and though the mountains be carried into the midst of the sea; 46:3 [Though] the waters thereof roar [and] be troubled, [though] the mountains shake with the swelling thereof. Selah. 46:4 [There is] a river, the streams whereof shall make glad the city of God, the holy [place] of the tabernacles of the most High. 46:5 God [is] in the midst of her; she shall not be moved: God shall help her, [and that] right early. 46:6 The heathen raged, the kingdoms were moved: he uttered his voice, the earth melted. 46:7 The LORD of hosts [is] with us; the God of Jacob [is] our refuge. Selah. 46:8 Come, behold the works of the LORD, what desolations he hath made in the earth. 46:9 He maketh wars to cease unto the end of the earth; he breaketh the bow, and cutteth the spear in sunder; he burneth the chariot in the fire. 46:10 Be still, and know that I [am] God: I will be exalted among the heathen, I will be exalted in the earth. 46:11 The LORD of hosts [is] with us; the God of Jacob [is] our refuge. Selah.

PSALM 47

To the chief Musician, A PSALM for the sons of Korah. 47:1 O clap your hands, all ye people; shout unto God with the voice of triumph. 47:2 For the LORD most high [is] terrible; [he is] a great King over all the earth. 47:3 He shall subdue the people under us, and the nations under our feet. 47:4 He shall choose our inheritance for us, the excellency of Jacob whom he loved. Selah. 47:5 God is gone up with a shout, the LORD with the sound of a trumpet. 47:6 Sing praises to God, sing praises: sing praises unto our King, sing praises. 47:7 For God [is] the King of all the earth: sing ye praises with understanding. 47:8 God reigneth over the heathen: God sitteth upon the throne of his holiness. 47:9 The princes of the people are gathered together, [even] the people of the God of Abraham: for the shields of the earth [belong] unto God: he is greatly exalted.

PSALM 48

A Song [and] PSALM for the sons of Korah. 48:1 Great [is] the LORD, and greatly to be praised in the city of our God, [in] the mountain of his holiness. 48:2 Beautiful for situation, the joy of the whole earth, [is] mount Zion, [on] the sides of the north, the city of the great King. 48:3 God is known in her palaces for a refuge. 48:4 For, lo, the kings were assembled, they passed by together. 48:5 They saw [it, and] so they marvelled; they were troubled, [and] hasted away. 48:6 Fear took hold upon them there, [and] pain, as of a woman in travail. 48:7 Thou breakest the shiof Tarshish with an east wind. 48:8 As we have heard, so have we seen in the city of the LORD of hosts, in the city of our God: God will establish it for ever. Selah. 48:9 We have thought of thy lovingkindness, O God, in the midst of thy temple. 48:10 According to thy name, O God, so [is] thy praise unto the ends of the earth: thy right hand is full of righteousness. 48:11 Let mount Zion rejoice, let the daughters of Judah be glad, because of thy judgments. 48:12 Walk about Zion, and go round about her: tell the towers thereof. 48:13 Mark ye well her bulwarks, consider her palaces; that ye may tell [it] to the generation following. 48:14 For this God [is] our God for ever and ever: he will be our guide [even] unto death.

PSALM 49
To the chief Musician, A PSALM for the sons of Korah. 49:1 Hear this, all [ye] people; give ear, all [ye] inhabitants of the world: 49:2 Both low and high, rich and poor, together. 49:3 My mouth shall speak of wisdom; and the meditation of my heart [shall be] of understanding. 49:4 I will incline mine ear to a parable: I will open my dark saying upon the harp. 49:5 Wherefore should I fear in the days of evil, [when] the iniquity of my heels shall compass me about? 49:6 They that trust in their wealth, and boast themselves in the multitude of their riches; 49:7 None [of them] can by any means redeem his brother, nor give to God a ransom for him: 49:8 (For the redemption of their soul [is] precious, and it ceaseth for ever:) 49:9 That he should still live for ever, [and] not see corruption. 49:10 For he seeth [that] wise men die, likewise the fool and the brutish person perish, and leave their wealth to others. 49:11 Their inward thought [is, that] their houses [shall continue] for ever, [and] their dwelling places to all generations; they call [their] lands after their own names. 49:12 Nevertheless man [being] in honour abideth not: he is like the beasts [that] perish. 49:13 This their way [is] their folly: yet their posterity approve their sayings. Selah. 49:14 Like sheep they are laid in the grave; death shall feed on them; and the upright shall have dominion over them in the morning; and their beauty shall consume in the grave from their dwelling. 49:15 But God will redeem my soul from the power of the grave: for he shall receive me. Selah. 49:16 Be not thou afraid when one is made rich, when the glory of his house is increased; 49:17 For when he dieth he shall carry nothing away: his glory shall not descend after him. 49:18 Though while he lived he blessed his soul: and [men] will praise thee, when thou

doest well to thyself. 49:19 He shall go to the generation of his fathers; they shall never see light. 49:20 Man [that is] in honour, and understandeth not, is like the beasts [that] perish.

PSALM 50

A PSALM of Asaph. 50:1 The mighty God, [even] the LORD, hath spoken, and called the earth from the rising of the sun unto the going down thereof. 50:2 Out of Zion, the perfection of beauty, God hath shined. 50:3 Our God shall come, and shall not keep silence: a fire shall devour before him, and it shall be very tempestuous round about him. 50:4 He shall call to the heavens from above, and to the earth, that he may judge his people. 50:5 Gather my saints together unto me; those that have made a covenant with me by sacrifice. 50:6 And the heavens shall declare his righteousness: for God [is] judge himself. Selah. 50:7 Hear, O my people, and I will speak; O Israel, and I will testify against thee: I [am] God, [even] thy God. 50:8 I will not reprove thee for thy sacrifices or thy burnt offerings, [to have been] continually before me. 50:9 I will take no bullock out of thy house, [nor] he goats out of thy folds. 50:10 For every beast of the forest [is] mine, [and] the cattle upon a thousand hills. 50:11 I know all the fowls of the mountains: and the wild beasts of the field [are] mine. 50:12 If I were hungry, I would not tell thee: for the world [is] mine, and the fulness thereof. 50:13 Will I eat the flesh of bulls, or drink the blood of goats? 50:14 Offer unto God thanksgiving; and pay thy vows unto the most High: 50:15 And call upon me in the day of trouble: I will deliver thee, and thou shalt glorify me. 50:16 But unto the wicked God saith, What hast thou to do to declare my statutes, or [that] thou shouldest take my covenant in thy mouth? 50:17 Seeing thou hatest instruction, and castest my words behind thee. 50:18 When thou sawest a thief, then thou consentedst with him, and hast been partaker with adulterers. 50:19 Thou givest thy mouth to evil, and thy tongue frameth deceit. 50:20 Thou sittest [and] speakest against thy brother; thou slanderest thine own mother's son. 50:21 These [things] hast thou done, and I kept silence; thou thoughtest that I was altogether [such an one] as thyself: [but]

I will reprove thee, and set [them] in order before thine eyes. 50:22 Now consider this, ye that forget God, lest I tear [you] in pieces, and [there be] none to deliver. 50:23 Whoso offereth praise glorifieth me: and to him that ordereth [his] conversation [aright] will I shew the salvation of God.

PSALM 51

To the chief Musician, A PSALM of David, when Nathan the prophet came unto him, after he had gone in to Bathsheba. 51:1 Have mercy upon me, O God, according to thy lovingkindness: according unto the multitude of thy tender mercies blot out my transgressions. 51:2 Wash me throughly from mine iniquity, and cleanse me from my sin. 51:3 For I acknowledge my transgressions: and my sin [is] ever before me. 51:4 Against thee, thee only, have I sinned, and done [this] evil in thy sight: that thou mightest be justified when thou speakest, [and] be clear when thou judgest. 51:5 Behold, I was shapen in iniquity; and in sin did my mother conceive me. 51:6 Behold, thou desirest truth in the inward parts: and in the hidden [part] thou shalt make me to know wisdom. 51:7 Purge me with hyssop, and I shall be clean: wash me, and I shall be whiter than snow. 51:8 Make me to hear joy and gladness; [that] the bones [which] thou hast broken may rejoice. 51:9 Hide thy face from my sins, and blot out all mine iniquities. 51:10 Create in me a clean heart, O God; and renew a right spirit within me. 51:11 Cast me not away from thy presence; and take not thy holy spirit from me. 51:12 Restore unto me the joy of thy salvation; and uphold me [with thy] free spirit. 51:13 [Then] will I teach transgressors thy ways; and sinners shall be converted unto thee. 51:14 Deliver me from bloodguiltiness, O God, thou God of my salvation: [and] my tongue shall sing aloud of thy righteousness. 51:15 O Lord, open thou my lips; and my mouth shall shew forth thy praise. 51:16 For thou desirest not sacrifice; else would I give [it]: thou delightest not in burnt offering. 51:17 The sacrifices of God [are] a broken spirit: a broken and a contrite heart, O God, thou wilt not despise. 51:18 Do good in thy good pleasure unto Zion: build thou the walls of Jerusalem. 51:19 Then shalt thou be pleased with the sacrifices of righteousness, with burnt offering and whole burnt offering: then shall they offer bullocks upon thine altar.

PSALM 52

To the chief Musician, Maschil, [A PSALM] of David, when Doeg the
Edomite came and told Saul, and said unto him, David is come to the house
of Ahimelech. 52:1 Why boastest thou thyself in mischief, O mighty man?
the goodness of God [endureth] continually. 52:2 Thy tongue deviseth
mischiefs; like a sharp rasor, working deceitfully. 52:3 Thou lovest evil more
than good; [and] lying rather than to speak righteousness. Selah. 52:4 Thou
lovest all devouring words, O [thou] deceitful tongue. 52:5 God shall likewise
destroy thee for ever, he shall take thee away, and pluck thee out of [thy]
dwelling place, and root thee out of the land of the living. Selah. 52:6 The
righteous also shall see, and fear, and shall laugh at him: 52:7 Lo, [this is] the
man [that] made not God his strength; but trusted in the abundance of his
riches, [and] strengthened himself in his wickedness. 52:8 But I [am] like a
green olive tree in the house of God: I trust in the mercy of God for ever and
ever. 52:9 I will praise thee for ever, because thou hast done [it]: and I will
wait on thy name; for [it is] good before thy saints.

PSALM 53

To the chief Musician upon Mahalath, Maschil, [A PSALM] of David. 53:1
The fool hath said in his heart, [There is] no God. Corrupt are they, and have
done abominable iniquity: [there is] none that doeth good. 53:2 God looked
down from heaven upon the children of men, to see if there were [any] that
did understand, that did seek God. 53:3 Every one of them is gone back: they
are altogether become filthy; [there is] none that doeth good, no, not one.
53:4 Have the workers of iniquity no knowledge? who eat up my people [as]
they eat bread: they have not called upon God. 53:5 There were they in great
fear, [where] no fear was: for God hath scattered the bones of him that
encampeth [against] thee: thou hast put [them] to shame, because God hath
despised them. 53:6 Oh that the salvation of Israel [were come] out of Zion!
When God bringeth back the captivity of his people, Jacob shall rejoice, [and]

Israel shall be glad.

PSALM 54
To the chief Musician on Neginoth, Maschil, [A PSALM] of David, when the
Ziphims came and said to Saul, Doth not David hide himself with us? 54:1
Save me, O God, by thy name, and judge me by thy strength. 54:2 Hear my
prayer, O God; give ear to the words of my mouth. 54:3 For strangers are
risen up against me, and oppressors seek after my soul: they have not set God
before them. Selah. 54:4 Behold, God [is] mine helper: the Lord [is] with
them that uphold my soul. 54:5 He shall reward evil unto mine enemies: cut
them off in thy truth. 54:6 I will freely sacrifice unto thee: I will praise thy
name, O LORD; for [it is] good. 54:7 For he hath delivered me out of all
trouble: and mine eye hath seen [his desire] upon mine enemies.

PSALM 55
To the chief Musician on Neginoth, Maschil, [A PSALM] of David. 55:1 Give
ear to my prayer, O God; and hide not thyself from my supplication. 55:2
Attend unto me, and hear me: I mourn in my complaint, and make a noise;
55:3 Because of the voice of the enemy, because of the oppression of the
wicked: for they cast iniquity upon me, and in wrath they hate me. 55:4 My
heart is sore pained within me: and the terrors of death are fallen upon me.
55:5 Fearfulness and trembling are come upon me, and horror hath
overwhelmed me. 55:6 And I said, Oh that I had wings like a dove! [for then]
would I fly away, and be at rest. 55:7 Lo, [then] would I wander far off, [and]
remain in the wilderness. Selah. 55:8 I would hasten my escape from the
windy storm [and] tempest. 55:9 Destroy, O Lord, [and] divide their tongues:
for I have seen violence and strife in the city. 55:10 Day and night they go
about it upon the walls thereof: mischief also and sorrow [are] in the midst
of it. 55:11 Wickedness [is] in the midst thereof: deceit and guile depart not
from her streets. 55:12 For [it was] not an enemy [that] reproached me; then
I could have borne [it]: neither [was it] he that hated me [that] did magnify
[himself] against me; then I would have hid myself from him: 55:13 But [it

was] thou, a man mine equal, my guide, and mine acquaintance. 55:14 We
took sweet counsel together, [and] walked unto the house of God in
company. 55:15 Let death seize upon them, [and] let them go down quick
into hell: for wickedness [is] in their dwellings, [and] among them. 55:16 As
for me, I will call upon God; and the LORD shall save me. 55:17 Evening,
and morning, and at noon, will I pray, and cry aloud: and he shall hear my
voice. 55:18 He hath delivered my soul in peace from the battle [that was]
against me: for there were many with me. 55:19 God shall hear, and afflict
them, even he that abideth of old. Selah. Because they have no changes,
therefore they fear not God. 55:20 He hath put forth his hands against such
as be at peace with him: he hath broken his covenant. 55:21 [The words] of
his mouth were smoother than butter, but war [was] in his heart: his words
were softer than oil, yet [were] they drawn swords. 55:22 Cast thy burden
upon the LORD, and he shall sustain thee: he shall never suffer the righteous
to be moved. 55:23 But thou, O God, shalt bring them down into the pit of
destruction: bloody and deceitful men shall not live out half their days; but
I will trust in thee.

PSALM 56
To the chief Musician upon Jonathelemrechokim, Michtam of David, when
the Philistines took him in Gath. 56:1 Be merciful unto me, O God: for man
would swallow me up; he fighting daily oppresseth me. 56:2 Mine enemies
would daily swallow [me] up: for [they be] many that fight against me, O thou
most High. 56:3 What time I am afraid, I will trust in thee. 56:4 In God I
will praise his word, in God I have put my trust; I will not fear what flesh can
do unto me. 56:5 Every day they wrest my words: all their thoughts [are]
against me for evil. 56:6 They gather themselves together, they hide
themselves, they mark my steps, when they wait for my soul. 56:7 Shall they
escape by iniquity? in [thine] anger cast down the people, O God. 56:8 Thou
tellest my wanderings: put thou my tears into thy bottle: [are they] not in thy
book? 56:9 When I cry [unto thee], then shall mine enemies turn back: this
I know; for God [is] for me. 56:10 In God will I praise [his] word: in the

LORD will I praise [his] word. 56:11 In God have I put my trust: I will not be afraid what man can do unto me. 56:12 Thy vows [are] upon me, O God: I will render praises unto thee. 56:13 For thou hast delivered my soul from death: [wilt] not [thou deliver] my feet from falling, that I may walk before God in the light of the living?

PSALM 57

To the chief Musician, Altaschith, Michtam of David, when he fled from Saul in the cave. 57:1 Be merciful unto me, O God, be merciful unto me: for my soul trusteth in thee: yea, in the shadow of thy wings will I make my refuge, until [these] calamities be overpast. 57:2 I will cry unto God most high; unto God that performeth [all things] for me. 57:3 He shall send from heaven, and save me [from] the reproach of him that would swallow me up. Selah. God shall send forth his mercy and his truth. 57:4 My soul [is] among lions: [and] I lie [even among] them that are set on fire, [even] the sons of men, whose teeth [are] spears and arrows, and their tongue a sharp sword. 57:5 Be thou exalted, O God, above the heavens; [let] thy glory [be] above all the earth. 57:6 They have prepared a net for my steps; my soul is bowed down: they have digged a pit before me, into the midst whereof they are fallen [themselves]. Selah. 57:7 My heart is fixed, O God, my heart is fixed: I will sing and give praise. 57:8 Awake up, my glory; awake, psaltery and harp: I [myself] will awake early. 57:9 I will praise thee, O Lord, among the people: I will sing unto thee among the nations. 57:10 For thy mercy [is] great unto the heavens, and thy truth unto the clouds. 57:11 Be thou exalted, O God, above the heavens: [let] thy glory [be] above all the earth.

PSALM 58

To the chief Musician, Altaschith, Michtam of David. 58:1 Do ye indeed speak righteousness, O congregation? do ye judge uprightly, O ye sons of men? 58:2 Yea, in heart ye work wickedness; ye weigh the violence of your hands in the earth. 58:3 The wicked are estranged from the womb: they go astray as soon as they be born, speaking lies. 58:4 Their poison [is] like the

poison of a serpent: [they are] like the deaf adder [that] stoppeth her ear; 58:5
Which will not hearken to the voice of charmers, charming never so wisely.
58:6 Break their teeth, O God, in their mouth: break out the great teeth of
the young lions, O LORD. 58:7 Let them melt away as waters [which] run
continually: [when] he bendeth [his bow to shoot] his arrows, let them be as
cut in pieces. 58:8 As a snail [which] melteth, let [every one of them] pass
away: [like] the untimely birth of a woman, [that] they may not see the sun.
58:9 Before your pots can feel the thorns, he shall take them away as with a
whirlwind, both living, and in [his] wrath. 58:10 The righteous shall rejoice
when he seeth the vengeance: he shall wash his feet in the blood of the
wicked. 58:11 So that a man shall say, Verily [there is] a reward for the
righteous: verily he is a God that judgeth in the earth.

PSALM 59

To the chief Musician, Altaschith, Michtam of David; when Saul sent, and
they watched the house to kill him. 59:1 Deliver me from mine enemies, O
my God: defend me from them that rise up against me. 59:2 Deliver me from
the workers of iniquity, and save me from bloody men. 59:3 For, lo, they lie
in wait for my soul: the mighty are gathered against me; not [for] my
transgression, nor [for] my sin, O LORD. 59:4 They run and prepare
themselves without [my] fault: awake to help me, and behold. 59:5 Thou
therefore, O LORD God of hosts, the God of Israel, awake to visit all the
heathen: be not merciful to any wicked transgressors. Selah. 59:6 They return
at evening: they make a noise like a dog, and go round about the city. 59:7
Behold, they belch out with their mouth: swords [are] in their lips: for who,
[say they], doth hear? 59:8 But thou, O LORD, shalt laugh at them; thou
shalt have all the heathen in derision. 59:9 [Because of] his strength will I
wait upon thee: for God [is] my defence. 59:10 The God of my mercy shall
prevent me: God shall let me see [my desire] upon mine enemies. 59:11 Slay
them not, lest my people forget: scatter them by thy power; and bring them
down, O Lord our shield. 59:12 [For] the sin of their mouth [and] the words
of their lilet them even be taken in their pride: and for cursing and lying

[which] they speak. 59:13 Consume [them] in wrath, consume [them], that they [may] not [be]: and let them know that God ruleth in Jacob unto the ends of the earth. Selah. 59:14 And at evening let them return; [and] let them make a noise like a dog, and go round about the city. 59:15 Let them wander up and down for meat, and grudge if they be not satisfied. 59:16 But I will sing of thy power; yea, I will sing aloud of thy mercy in the morning: for thou hast been my defence and refuge in the day of my trouble. 59:17 Unto thee, O my strength, will I sing: for God [is] my defence, [and] the God of my mercy.

PSALM 60

To the chief Musician upon Shushaneduth, Michtam of David, to teach; when he strove with Aramnaharaim and with Aramzobah, when Joab returned, and smote of Edom in the valley of salt twelve thousand. 60:1 O God, thou hast cast us off, thou hast scattered us, thou hast been displeased; O turn thyself to us again. 60:2 Thou hast made the earth to tremble; thou hast broken it: heal the breaches thereof; for it shaketh. 60:3 Thou hast shewed thy people hard things: thou hast made us to drink the wine of astonishment. 60:4 Thou hast given a banner to them that fear thee, that it may be displayed because of the truth. Selah. 60:5 That thy beloved may be delivered; save [with] thy right hand, and hear me. 60:6 God hath spoken in his holiness; I will rejoice, I will divide Shechem, and mete out the valley of Succoth. 60:7 Gilead [is] mine, and Manasseh [is] mine; Ephraim also [is] the strength of mine head; Judah [is] my lawgiver; 60:8 Moab [is] my washpot; over Edom will I cast out my shoe: Philistia, triumph thou because of me. 60:9 Who will bring me [into] the strong city? who will lead me into Edom? 60:10 [Wilt] not thou, O God, [which] hadst cast us off? and [thou], O God, [which] didst not go out with our armies? 60:11 Give us help from trouble: for vain [is] the help of man. 60:12 Through God we shall do valiantly: for he [it is that] shall tread down our enemies.

PSALMS

PSALM 61

To the chief Musician upon Neginah, [A PSALM] of David. 61:1 Hear my cry, O God; attend unto my prayer. 61:2 From the end of the earth will I cry unto thee, when my heart is overwhelmed: lead me to the rock [that] is higher than I. 61:3 For thou hast been a shelter for me, [and] a strong tower from the enemy. 61:4 I will abide in thy tabernacle for ever: I will trust in the covert of thy wings. Selah. 61:5 For thou, O God, hast heard my vows: thou hast given [me] the heritage of those that fear thy name. 61:6 Thou wilt prolong the king's life: [and] his years as many generations. 61:7 He shall abide before God for ever: O prepare mercy and truth, [which] may preserve him. 61:8 So will I sing praise unto thy name for ever, that I may daily perform my vows.

PSALM 62

To the chief Musician, to Jeduthun, A PSALM of David. 62:1 Truly my soul waiteth upon God: from him [cometh] my salvation. 62:2 He only [is] my rock and my salvation; [he is] my defence; I shall not be greatly moved. 62:3 How long will ye imagine mischief against a man? ye shall be slain all of you: as a bowing wall [shall ye be, and as] a tottering fence. 62:4 They only consult to cast [him] down from his excellency: they delight in lies: they bless with their mouth, but they curse inwardly. Selah. 62:5 My soul, wait thou only upon God; for my expectation [is] from him. 62:6 He only [is] my rock and my salvation: [he is] my defence; I shall not be moved. 62:7 In God [is] my salvation and my glory: the rock of my strength, [and] my refuge, [is] in God. 62:8 Trust in him at all times; ye people, pour out your heart before him: God [is] a refuge for us. Selah. 62:9 Surely men of low degree [are] vanity, [and] men of high degree [are] a lie: to be laid in the balance, they [are] altogether [lighter] than vanity. 62:10 Trust not in oppression, and become not vain in robbery: if riches increase, set not your heart [upon them]. 62:11 God hath spoken once; twice have I heard this; that power [belongeth] unto God. 62:12 Also unto thee, O Lord, [belongeth] mercy: for thou renderest to every man according to his work.

PSALM 63

A PSALM of David, when he was in the wilderness of Judah. 63:1 O God, thou [art] my God; early will I seek thee: my soul thirsteth for thee, my flesh longeth for thee in a dry and thirsty land, where no water is; 63:2 To see thy power and thy glory, so [as] I have seen thee in the sanctuary. 63:3 Because thy lovingkindness [is] better than life, my lishall praise thee. 63:4 Thus will I bless thee while I live: I will lift up my hands in thy name. 63:5 My soul shall be satisfied as [with] marrow and fatness; and my mouth shall praise [thee] with joyful lips: 63:6 When I remember thee upon my bed, [and] meditate on thee in the [night] watches. 63:7 Because thou hast been my help, therefore in the shadow of thy wings will I rejoice. 63:8 My soul followeth hard after thee: thy right hand upholdeth me. 63:9 But those [that] seek my soul, to destroy [it], shall go into the lower parts of the earth. 63:10 They shall fall by the sword: they shall be a portion for foxes. 63:11 But the king shall rejoice in God; every one that sweareth by him shall glory: but the mouth of them that speak lies shall be stopped.

PSALM 64

To the chief Musician, A PSALM of David. 64:1 Hear my voice, O God, in my prayer: preserve my life from fear of the enemy. 64:2 Hide me from the secret counsel of the wicked; from the insurrection of the workers of iniquity: 64:3 Who whet their tongue like a sword, [and] bend [their bows to shoot] their arrows, [even] bitter words: 64:4 That they may shoot in secret at the perfect: suddenly do they shoot at him, and fear not. 64:5 They encourage themselves [in] an evil matter: they commune of laying snares privily; they say, Who shall see them? 64:6 They search out iniquities; they accomplish a diligent search: both the inward [thought] of every one [of them], and the heart, [is] deep. 64:7 But God shall shoot at them [with] an arrow; suddenly shall they be wounded. 64:8 So they shall make their own tongue to fall upon themselves: all that see them shall flee away. 64:9 And all men shall fear, and shall declare the work of God; for they shall wisely consider of his doing. 64:10 The righteous shall be glad in the LORD, and shall trust in him; and all the upright in heart shall glory.

PSALM 65

To the chief Musician, A PSALM [and] Song of David. 65:1 Praise waiteth for thee, O God, in Sion: and unto thee shall the vow be performed. 65:2 O thou that hearest prayer, unto thee shall all flesh come. 65:3 Iniquities prevail against me: [as for] our transgressions, thou shalt purge them away. 65:4 Blessed [is the man whom] thou choosest, and causest to approach [unto thee, that] he may dwell in thy courts: we shall be satisfied with the goodness of thy house, [even] of thy holy temple. 65:5 [By] terrible things in righteousness wilt thou answer us, O God of our salvation; [who art] the confidence of all the ends of the earth, and of them that are afar off [upon] the sea: 65:6 Which by his strength setteth fast the mountains; [being] girded with power: 65:7 Which stilleth the noise of the seas, the noise of their waves, and the tumult of the people. 65:8 They also that dwell in the uttermost parts are afraid at thy tokens: thou makest the outgoings of the morning and evening to rejoice. 65:9 Thou visitest the earth, and waterest it: thou greatly enrichest it with the river of God, [which] is full of water: thou preparest them corn, when thou hast so provided for it. 65:10 Thou waterest the ridges thereof abundantly: thou settlest the furrows thereof: thou makest it soft with showers: thou blessest the springing thereof. 65:11 Thou crownest the year with thy goodness; and thy paths drop fatness. 65:12 They drop [upon] the pastures of the wilderness: and the little hills rejoice on every side. 65:13 The pastures are clothed with flocks; the valleys also are covered over with corn; they shout for joy, they also sing.

PSALM 66

To the chief Musician, A Song [or] PSALM. 66:1 Make a joyful noise unto God, all ye lands: 66:2 Sing forth the honour of his name: make his praise glorious. 66:3 Say unto God, How terrible [art thou in] thy works! through the greatness of thy power shall thine enemies submit themselves unto thee. 66:4 All the earth shall worship thee, and shall sing unto thee; they shall sing

[to] thy name. Selah. 66:5 Come and see the works of God: [he is] terrible [in his] doing toward the children of men. 66:6 He turned the sea into dry [land]: they went through the flood on foot: there did we rejoice in him. 66:7 He ruleth by his power for ever; his eyes behold the nations: let not the rebellious exalt themselves. Selah. 66:8 O bless our God, ye people, and make the voice of his praise to be heard: 66:9 Which holdeth our soul in life, and suffereth not our feet to be moved. 66:10 For thou, O God, hast proved us: thou hast tried us, as silver is tried. 66:11 Thou broughtest us into the net; thou laidst affliction upon our loins. 66:12 Thou hast caused men to ride over our heads; we went through fire and through water: but thou broughtest us out into a wealthy [place]. 66:13 I will go into thy house with burnt offerings: I will pay thee my vows, 66:14 Which my lihave uttered, and my mouth hath spoken, when I was in trouble. 66:15 I will offer unto thee burnt sacrifices of fatlings, with the incense of rams; I will offer bullocks with goats. Selah. 66:16 Come [and] hear, all ye that fear God, and I will declare what he hath done for my soul. 66:17 I cried unto him with my mouth, and he was extolled with my tongue. 66:18 If I regard iniquity in my heart, the Lord will not hear [me]: 66:19 [But] verily God hath heard [me]; he hath attended to the voice of my prayer. 66:20 Blessed [be] God, which hath not turned away my prayer, nor his mercy from me.

PSALM 67

To the chief Musician on Neginoth, A PSALM [or] Song. 67:1 God be merciful unto us, and bless us; [and] cause his face to shine upon us; Selah. 67:2 That thy way may be known upon earth, thy saving health among all nations. 67:3 Let the people praise thee, O God; let all the people praise thee. 67:4 O let the nations be glad and sing for joy: for thou shalt judge the people righteously, and govern the nations upon earth. Selah. 67:5 Let the people praise thee, O God; let all the people praise thee. 67:6 [Then] shall the earth yield her increase; [and] God, [even] our own God, shall bless us. 67:7 God shall bless us; and all the ends of the earth shall fear him.

PSALMS

PSALM 68

To the chief Musician, A PSALM [or] Song of David. 68:1 Let God arise, let his enemies be scattered: let them also that hate him flee before him. 68:2 As smoke is driven away, [so] drive [them] away: as wax melteth before the fire, [so] let the wicked perish at the presence of God. 68:3 But let the righteous be glad; let them rejoice before God: yea, let them exceedingly rejoice. 68:4 Sing unto God, sing praises to his name: extol him that rideth upon the heavens by his name JAH, and rejoice before him. 68:5 A father of the fatherless, and a judge of the widows, [is] God in his holy habitation. 68:6 God setteth the solitary in families: he bringeth out those which are bound with chains: but the rebellious dwell in a dry [land]. 68:7 O God, when thou wentest forth before thy people, when thou didst march through the wilderness; Selah: 68:8 The earth shook, the heavens also dropped at the presence of God: [even] Sinai itself [was moved] at the presence of God, the God of Israel. 68:9 Thou, O God, didst send a plentiful rain, whereby thou didst confirm thine inheritance, when it was weary. 68:10 Thy congregation hath dwelt therein: thou, O God, hast prepared of thy goodness for the poor. 68:11 The Lord gave the word: great [was] the company of those that published [it]. 68:12 Kings of armies did flee apace: and she that tarried at home divided the spoil. 68:13 Though ye have lien among the pots, [yet shall ye be as] the wings of a dove covered with silver, and her feathers with yellow gold. 68:14 When the Almighty scattered kings in it, it was [white] as snow in Salmon. 68:15 The hill of God [is as] the hill of Bashan; an high hill [as] the hill of Bashan. 68:16 Why leap ye, ye high hills? [this is] the hill [which] God desireth to dwell in; yea, the LORD will dwell [in it] for ever. 68:17 The chariots of God [are] twenty thousand, [even] thousands of angels: the Lord [is] among them, [as in] Sinai, in the holy [place]. 68:18 Thou hast ascended on high, thou hast led captivity captive: thou hast received gifts for men; yea, [for] the rebellious also, that the LORD God might dwell [among them]. 68:19 Blessed [be] the Lord, [who] daily loadeth us [with benefits, even] the God of our salvation. Selah. 68:20 [He that is] our God [is] the God of salvation; and unto GOD the Lord [belong] the issues from death. 68:21 But

God shall wound the head of his enemies, [and] the hairy scalp of such an one as goeth on still in his trespasses. 68:22 The Lord said, I will bring again from Bashan, I will bring [my people] again from the depths of the sea: 68:23 That thy foot may be dipped in the blood of [thine] enemies, [and] the tongue of thy dogs in the same. 68:24 They have seen thy goings, O God; [even] the goings of my God, my King, in the sanctuary. 68:25 The singers went before, the players on instruments [followed] after; among [them were] the damsels playing with timbrels. 68:26 Bless ye God in the congregations, [even] the Lord, from the fountain of Israel. 68:27 There [is] little Benjamin [with] their ruler, the princes of Judah [and] their council, the princes of Zebulun, [and] the princes of Naphtali. 68:28 Thy God hath commanded thy strength: strengthen, O God, that which thou hast wrought for us. 68:29 Because of thy temple at Jerusalem shall kings bring presents unto thee. 68:30 Rebuke the company of spearmen, the multitude of the bulls, with the calves of the people, [till every one] submit himself with pieces of silver: scatter thou the people [that] delight in war. 68:31 Princes shall come out of Egypt; Ethiopia shall soon stretch out her hands unto God. 68:32 Sing unto God, ye kingdoms of the earth; O sing praises unto the Lord; Selah: 68:33 To him that rideth upon the heavens of heavens, [which were] of old; lo, he doth send out his voice, [and that] a mighty voice. 68:34 Ascribe ye strength unto God: his excellency [is] over Israel, and his strength [is] in the clouds. 68:35 O God, [thou art] terrible out of thy holy places: the God of Israel [is] he that giveth strength and power unto [his] people. Blessed [be] God.

PSALM 69

To the chief Musician upon Shoshannim, [A PSALM] of David. 69:1 Save me, O God; for the waters are come in unto [my] soul. 69:2 I sink in deep mire, where [there is] no standing: I am come into deep waters, where the floods overflow me. 69:3 I am weary of my crying: my throat is dried: mine eyes fail while I wait for my God. 69:4 They that hate me without a cause are more than the hairs of mine head: they that would destroy me, [being] mine enemies wrongfully, are mighty: then I restored [that] which I took not away.

69:5 O God, thou knowest my foolishness; and my sins are not hid from
thee. 69:6 Let not them that wait on thee, O Lord GOD of hosts, be
ashamed for my sake: let not those that seek thee be confounded for my sake,
O God of Israel. 69:7 Because for thy sake I have borne reproach; shame
hath covered my face. 69:8 I am become a stranger unto my brethren, and an
alien unto my mother's children. 69:9 For the zeal of thine house hath eaten
me up; and the reproaches of them that reproached thee are fallen upon me.
69:10 When I wept, [and chastened] my soul with fasting, that was to my
reproach. 69:11 I made sackcloth also my garment; and I became a proverb
to them. 69:12 They that sit in the gate speak against me; and I [was] the song
of the drunkards. 69:13 But as for me, my prayer [is] unto thee, O LORD,
[in] an acceptable time: O God, in the multitude of thy mercy hear me, in the
truth of thy salvation. 69:14 Deliver me out of the mire, and let me not sink:
let me be delivered from them that hate me, and out of the deep waters.
69:15 Let not the waterflood overflow me, neither let the deep swallow me
up, and let not the pit shut her mouth upon me. 69:16 Hear me, O LORD;
for thy lovingkindness [is] good: turn unto me according to the multitude of
thy tender mercies. 69:17 And hide not thy face from thy servant; for I am
in trouble: hear me speedily. 69:18 Draw nigh unto my soul, [and] redeem
it: deliver me because of mine enemies. 69:19 Thou hast known my
reproach, and my shame, and my dishonour: mine adversaries [are] all before
thee. 69:20 Reproach hath broken my heart; and I am full of heaviness: and
I looked [for some] to take pity, but [there was] none; and for comforters, but
I found none. 69:21 They gave me also gall for my meat; and in my thirst
they gave me vinegar to drink. 69:22 Let their table become a snare before
them: and [that which should have been] for [their] welfare, [let it become]
a trap. 69:23 Let their eyes be darkened, that they see not; and make their
loins continually to shake. 69:24 Pour out thine indignation upon them, and
let thy wrathful anger take hold of them. 69:25 Let their habitation be
desolate; [and] let none dwell in their tents. 69:26 For they persecute [him]
whom thou hast smitten; and they talk to the grief of those whom thou hast
wounded. 69:27 Add iniquity unto their iniquity: and let them not come

into thy righteousness. 69:28 Let them be blotted out of the book of the
living, and not be written with the righteous. 69:29 But I [am] poor and
sorrowful: let thy salvation, O God, set me up on high. 69:30 I will praise the
name of God with a song, and will magnify him with thanksgiving. 69:31
[This] also shall please the LORD better than an ox [or] bullock that hath
horns and hoofs. 69:32 The humble shall see [this, and] be glad: and your
heart shall live that seek God. 69:33 For the LORD heareth the poor, and
despiseth not his prisoners. 69:34 Let the heaven and earth praise him, the
seas, and every thing that moveth therein. 69:35 For God will save Zion, and
will build the cities of Judah: that they may dwell there, and have it in
possession. 69:36 The seed also of his servants shall inherit it: and they that
love his name shall dwell therein.

PSALM 70

To the chief Musician, [A PSALM] of David, to bring to remembrance. 70:1
[Make haste], O God, to deliver me; make haste to help me, O LORD. 70:2
Let them be ashamed and confounded that seek after my soul: let them be
turned backward, and put to confusion, that desire my hurt. 70:3 Let them
be turned back for a reward of their shame that say, Aha, aha. 70:4 Let all
those that seek thee rejoice and be glad in thee: and let such as love thy
salvation say continually, Let God be magnified. 70:5 But I [am] poor and
needy: make haste unto me, O God: thou [art] my help and my deliverer; O
LORD, make no tarrying.

PSALM 71

71:1 In thee, O LORD, do I put my trust: let me never be put to confusion.
71:2 Deliver me in thy righteousness, and cause me to escape: incline thine
ear unto me, and save me. 71:3 Be thou my strong habitation, whereunto I
may continually resort: thou hast given commandment to save me; for thou
[art] my rock and my fortress. 71:4 Deliver me, O my God, out of the hand
of the wicked, out of the hand of the unrighteous and cruel man. 71:5 For
thou [art] my hope, O Lord GOD: [thou art] my trust from my youth. 71:6

By thee have I been holden up from the womb: thou art he that took me out of my mother's bowels: my praise [shall be] continually of thee. 71:7 I am as a wonder unto many; but thou [art] my strong refuge. 71:8 Let my mouth be filled [with] thy praise [and with] thy honour all the day. 71:9 Cast me not off in the time of old age; forsake me not when my strength faileth. 71:10 For mine enemies speak against me; and they that lay wait for my soul take counsel together, 71:11 Saying, God hath forsaken him: persecute and take him; for [there is] none to deliver [him]. 71:12 O God, be not far from me: O my God, make haste for my help. 71:13 Let them be confounded [and] consumed that are adversaries to my soul; let them be covered [with] reproach and dishonour that seek my hurt. 71:14 But I will hope continually, and will yet praise thee more and more. 71:15 My mouth shall shew forth thy righteousness [and] thy salvation all the day; for I know not the numbers [thereof]. 71:16 I will go in the strength of the Lord GOD: I will make mention of thy righteousness, [even] of thine only. 71:17 O God, thou hast taught me from my youth: and hitherto have I declared thy wondrous works. 71:18 Now also when I am old and grayheaded, O God, forsake me not; until I have shewed thy strength unto [this] generation, [and] thy power to every one [that] is to come. 71:19 Thy righteousness also, O God, [is] very high, who hast done great things: O God, who [is] like unto thee! 71:20 [Thou], which hast shewed me great and sore troubles, shalt quicken me again, and shalt bring me up again from the depths of the earth. 71:21 Thou shalt increase my greatness, and comfort me on every side. 71:22 I will also praise thee with the psaltery, [even] thy truth, O my God: unto thee will I sing with the harp, O thou Holy One of Israel. 71:23 My lishall greatly rejoice when I sing unto thee; and my soul, which thou hast redeemed. 71:24 My tongue also shall talk of thy righteousness all the day long: for they are confounded, for they are brought unto shame, that seek my hurt.

PSALM 72

[A PSALM] for Solomon. 72:1 Give the king thy judgments, O God, and thy righteousness unto the king's son. 72:2 He shall judge thy people with righteousness, and thy poor with judgment. 72:3 The mountains shall bring peace to the people, and the little hills, by righteousness. 72:4 He shall judge the poor of the people, he shall save the children of the needy, and shall break in pieces the oppressor. 72:5 They shall fear thee as long as the sun and moon endure, throughout all generations. 72:6 He shall come down like rain upon the mown grass: as showers [that] water the earth. 72:7 In his days shall the righteous flourish; and abundance of peace so long as the moon endureth. 72:8 He shall have dominion also from sea to sea, and from the river unto the ends of the earth. 72:9 They that dwell in the wilderness shall bow before him; and his enemies shall lick the dust. 72:10 The kings of Tarshish and of the isles shall bring presents: the kings of Sheba and Seba shall offer gifts. 72:11 Yea, all kings shall fall down before him: all nations shall serve him. 72:12 For he shall deliver the needy when he crieth; the poor also, and [him] that hath no helper. 72:13 He shall spare the poor and needy, and shall save the souls of the needy. 72:14 He shall redeem their soul from deceit and violence: and precious shall their blood be in his sight. 72:15 And he shall live, and to him shall be given of the gold of Sheba: prayer also shall be made for him continually; [and] daily shall he be praised. 72:16 There shall be an handful of corn in the earth upon the top of the mountains; the fruit thereof shall shake like Lebanon: and [they] of the city shall flourish like grass of the earth. 72:17 His name shall endure for ever: his name shall be continued as long as the sun: and [men] shall be blessed in him: all nations shall call him blessed. 72:18 Blessed [be] the LORD God, the God of Israel, who only doeth wondrous things. 72:19 And blessed [be] his glorious name for ever: and let the whole earth be filled [with] his glory; Amen, and Amen. 72:20 The prayers of David the son of Jesse are ended.

PSALM 73

A PSALM of Asaph. 73:1 Truly God [is] good to Israel, [even] to such as are of a clean heart. 73:2 But as for me, my feet were almost gone; my stehad well nigh slipped. 73:3 For I was envious at the foolish, [when] I saw the prosperity of the wicked. 73:4 For [there are] no bands in their death: but their strength [is] firm. 73:5 They [are] not in trouble [as other] men; neither are they plagued like [other] men. 73:6 Therefore pride compasseth them about as a chain; violence covereth them [as] a garment. 73:7 Their eyes stand out with fatness: they have more than heart could wish. 73:8 They are corrupt, and speak wickedly [concerning] oppression: they speak loftily. 73:9 They set their mouth against the heavens, and their tongue walketh through the earth. 73:10 Therefore his people return hither: and waters of a full [cup] are wrung out to them. 73:11 And they say, How doth God know? and is there knowledge in the most High? 73:12 Behold, these [are] the ungodly, who prosper in the world; they increase [in] riches. 73:13 Verily I have cleansed my heart [in] vain, and washed my hands in innocency. 73:14 For all the day long have I been plagued, and chastened every morning. 73:15 If I say, I will speak thus; behold, I should offend [against] the generation of thy children. 73:16 When I thought to know this, it [was] too painful for me; 73:17 Until I went into the sanctuary of God; [then] understood I their end. 73:18 Surely thou didst set them in slippery places: thou castedst them down into destruction. 73:19 How are they [brought] into desolation, as in a moment! they are utterly consumed with terrors. 73:20 As a dream when [one] awaketh; [so], O Lord, when thou awakest, thou shalt despise their image. 73:21 Thus my heart was grieved, and I was pricked in my reins. 73:22 So foolish [was] I, and ignorant: I was [as] a beast before thee. 73:23 Nevertheless I [am] continually with thee: thou hast holden [me] by my right hand. 73:24 Thou shalt guide me with thy counsel, and afterward receive me [to] glory. 73:25 Whom have I in heaven [but thee]? and [there is] none upon earth [that] I desire beside thee. 73:26 My flesh and my heart faileth: [but] God [is] the strength of my heart, and my portion for ever. 73:27 For, lo, they that are far from thee shall perish: thou hast destroyed all them that go a whoring from thee. 73:28 But [it is] good for me to draw near to God: I have put my trust in the Lord GOD, that I may declare all thy works.

PSALM 74

Maschil of Asaph. 74:1 O God, why hast thou cast [us] off for ever? [why]

doth thine anger smoke against the sheep of thy pasture? 74:2 Remember thy congregation, [which] thou hast purchased of old; the rod of thine inheritance, [which] thou hast redeemed; this mount Zion, wherein thou hast dwelt. 74:3 Lift up thy feet unto the perpetual desolations; [even] all [that] the enemy hath done wickedly in the sanctuary. 74:4 Thine enemies roar in the midst of thy congregations; they set up their ensigns [for] signs. 74:5 [A man] was famous according as he had lifted up axes upon the thick trees. 74:6 But now they break down the carved work thereof at once with axes and hammers. 74:7 They have cast fire into thy sanctuary, they have defiled [by casting down] the dwelling place of thy name to the ground. 74:8 They said in their hearts, Let us destroy them together: they have burned up all the synagogues of God in the land. 74:9 We see not our signs: [there is] no more any prophet: neither [is there] among us any that knoweth how long. 74:10 O God, how long shall the adversary reproach? shall the enemy blaspheme thy name for ever? 74:11 Why withdrawest thou thy hand, even thy right hand? pluck [it] out of thy bosom. 74:12 For God [is] my King of old, working salvation in the midst of the earth. 74:13 Thou didst divide the sea by thy strength: thou brakest the heads of the dragons in the waters. 74:14 Thou brakest the heads of leviathan in pieces, [and] gavest him [to be] meat to the people inhabiting the wilderness. 74:15 Thou didst cleave the fountain and the flood: thou driedst up mighty rivers. 74:16 The day [is] thine, the night also [is] thine: thou hast prepared the light and the sun. 74:17 Thou hast set all the borders of the earth: thou hast made summer and winter. 74:18 Remember this, [that] the enemy hath reproached, O LORD, and [that] the foolish people have blasphemed thy name. 74:19 O deliver not the soul of thy turtledove unto the multitude [of the wicked]: forget not the congregation of thy poor for ever. 74:20 Have respect unto the covenant: for the dark places of the earth are full of the habitations of cruelty. 74:21 O let not the oppressed return ashamed: let the poor and needy praise thy name. 74:22 Arise, O God, plead thine own cause: remember how the foolish man reproacheth thee daily. 74:23 Forget not the voice of thine enemies: the tumult of those that rise up against thee increaseth continually.

PSALM 75

To the chief Musician, Altaschith, A PSALM [or] Song of Asaph. 75:1 Unto thee, O God, do we give thanks, [unto thee] do we give thanks: for [that] thy name is near thy wondrous works declare. 75:2 When I shall receive the congregation I will judge uprightly. 75:3 The earth and all the inhabitants thereof are dissolved: I bear up the pillars of it. Selah. 75:4 I said unto the fools, Deal not foolishly: and to the wicked, Lift not up the horn: 75:5 Lift not up your horn on high: speak [not with] a stiff neck. 75:6 For promotion [cometh] neither from the east, nor from the west, nor from the south. 75:7 But God [is] the judge: he putteth down one, and setteth up another. 75:8 For in the hand of the LORD [there is] a cup, and the wine is red; it is full of mixture; and he poureth out of the same: but the dregs thereof, all the wicked of the earth shall wring [them] out, [and] drink [them]. 75:9 But I will declare for ever; I will sing praises to the God of Jacob. 75:10 All the horns of the wicked also will I cut off; [but] the horns of the righteous shall be exalted.

PSALM 76

To the chief Musician on Neginoth, A PSALM [or] Song of Asaph. 76:1 In Judah [is] God known: his name [is] great in Israel. 76:2 In Salem also is his tabernacle, and his dwelling place in Zion. 76:3 There brake he the arrows of the bow, the shield, and the sword, and the battle. Selah. 76:4 Thou [art] more glorious [and] excellent than the mountains of prey. 76:5 The stouthearted are spoiled, they have slept their sleep: and none of the men of might have found their hands. 76:6 At thy rebuke, O God of Jacob, both the chariot and horse are cast into a dead sleep. 76:7 Thou, [even] thou, [art] to be feared: and who may stand in thy sight when once thou art angry? 76:8 Thou didst cause judgment to be heard from heaven; the earth feared, and was still, 76:9 When God arose to judgment, to save all the meek of the earth. Selah. 76:10 Surely the wrath of man shall praise thee: the remainder of wrath shalt thou restrain. 76:11 Vow, and pay unto the LORD your God: let all that be round about him bring presents unto him that ought to be

feared. 76:12 He shall cut off the spirit of princes: [he is] terrible to the kings
of the earth.

PSALM 77

To the chief Musician, to Jeduthun, A PSALM of Asaph. 77:1 I cried unto
God with my voice, [even] unto God with my voice; and he gave ear unto me.
77:2 In the day of my trouble I sought the Lord: my sore ran in the night,
and ceased not: my soul refused to be comforted. 77:3 I remembered God,
and was troubled: I complained, and my spirit was overwhelmed. Selah. 77:4
Thou holdest mine eyes waking: I am so troubled that I cannot speak. 77:5
I have considered the days of old, the years of ancient times. 77:6 I call to
remembrance my song in the night: I commune with mine own heart: and
my spirit made diligent search. 77:7 Will the Lord cast off for ever? and will
he be favourable no more? 77:8 Is his mercy clean gone for ever? doth [his]
promise fail for evermore? 77:9 Hath God forgotten to be gracious? hath he
in anger shut up his tender mercies? Selah. 77:10 And I said, This [is] my
infirmity: [but I will remember] the years of the right hand of the most High.
77:11 I will remember the works of the LORD: surely I will remember thy
wonders of old. 77:12 I will meditate also of all thy work, and talk of thy
doings. 77:13 Thy way, O God, [is] in the sanctuary: who [is so] great a God
as [our] God? 77:14 Thou [art] the God that doest wonders: thou hast
declared thy strength among the people. 77:15 Thou hast with [thine] arm
redeemed thy people, the sons of Jacob and Joseph. Selah. 77:16 The waters
saw thee, O God, the waters saw thee; they were afraid: the depths also were
troubled. 77:17 The clouds poured out water: the skies sent out a sound:
thine arrows also went abroad. 77:18 The voice of thy thunder [was] in the
heaven: the lightnings lightened the world: the earth trembled and shook.
77:19 Thy way [is] in the sea, and thy path in the great waters, and thy
footsteare not known. 77:20 Thou leddest thy people like a flock by the hand
of Moses and Aaron.

PSALMS

PSALM 78

Maschil of Asaph. 78:1 Give ear, O my people, [to] my law: incline your ears to the words of my mouth. 78:2 I will open my mouth in a parable: I will utter dark sayings of old: 78:3 Which we have heard and known, and our fathers have told us. 78:4 We will not hide [them] from their children, shewing to the generation to come the praises of the LORD, and his strength, and his wonderful works that he hath done. 78:5 For he established a testimony in Jacob, and appointed a law in Israel, which he commanded our fathers, that they should make them known to their children: 78:6 That the generation to come might know [them, even] the children [which] should be born; [who] should arise and declare [them] to their children: 78:7 That they might set their hope in God, and not forget the works of God, but keep his commandments: 78:8 And might not be as their fathers, a stubborn and rebellious generation; a generation [that] set not their heart aright, and whose spirit was not stedfast with God. 78:9 The children of Ephraim, [being] armed, [and] carrying bows, turned back in the day of battle. 78:10 They kept not the covenant of God, and refused to walk in his law; 78:11 And forgat his works, and his wonders that he had shewed them. 78:12 Marvellous things did he in the sight of their fathers, in the land of Egypt, [in] the field of Zoan. 78:13 He divided the sea, and caused them to pass through; and he made the waters to stand as an heap. 78:14 In the daytime also he led them with a cloud, and all the night with a light of fire. 78:15 He clave the rocks in the wilderness, and gave [them] drink as [out of] the great depths. 78:16 He brought streams also out of the rock, and caused waters to run down like rivers. 78:17 And they sinned yet more against him by provoking the most High in the wilderness. 78:18 And they tempted God in their heart by asking meat for their lust. 78:19 Yea, they spake against God; they said, Can God furnish a table in the wilderness? 78:20 Behold, he smote the rock, that the waters gushed out, and the streams overflowed; can he give bread also? can he provide flesh for his people? 78:21 Therefore the LORD heard [this], and was wroth: so a fire was kindled against Jacob, and anger also came up against Israel; 78:22 Because they believed not in God, and trusted not in his salvation: 78:23 Though he had commanded the clouds from above, and opened the doors of heaven, 78:24 And had rained down manna upon them to eat, and had given them of the corn of heaven. 78:25 Man did eat angels' food: he sent them meat to the full. 78:26 He caused an east wind to blow in the heaven: and by his power he brought in the south wind. 78:27 He rained flesh also upon them as dust, and feathered fowls like as the sand of the sea: 78:28 And he let [it] fall in the midst of their camp, round about their habitations. 78:29 So they did eat, and were well filled: for he gave them their own desire; 78:30 They were not estranged from their lust. But while their meat [was] yet in their mouths, 78:31 The wrath of God came upon them, and slew the fattest of them, and smote down the chosen [men] of Israel. 78:32 For all this they sinned still, and believed not for his wondrous works. 78:33 Therefore their days did he consume in vanity, and their years in trouble. 78:34 When he slew them, then they sought him: and they returned and inquired early after God. 78:35 And they remembered that God [was] their rock, and the high God their redeemer. 78:36 Nevertheless they did flatter him with their mouth, and they lied unto him with their tongues. 78:37 For their heart was not right with him, neither were they stedfast in his covenant. 78:38 But he, [being] full of compassion, forgave [their] iniquity, and destroyed [them] not: yea, many a time turned he his anger away, and did not stir up all his wrath. 78:39 For he remembered that they [were but] flesh; a wind that passeth away, and cometh not again. 78:40 How oft did they provoke him in the wilderness, [and] grieve him in the desert! 78:41 Yea, they turned back and tempted God, and limited the Holy One of Israel. 78:42 They remembered not his hand, [nor] the day when he delivered them from the enemy. 78:43 How he had wrought his signs in Egypt, and his wonders in the field of Zoan: 78:44 And had turned their rivers into blood; and their floods, that they could not drink. 78:45 He sent divers sorts of flies among them, which devoured them; and frogs, which destroyed them. 78:46 He gave also their increase unto the caterpiller, and their labour unto the locust. 78:47 He destroyed their vines with hail, and their sycomore trees with frost. 78:48 He gave up their cattle also to the hail, and their flocks to hot

thunderbolts. 78:49 He cast upon them the fierceness of his anger, wrath,
and indignation, and trouble, by sending evil angels [among them]. 78:50 He
made a way to his anger; he spared not their soul from death, but gave their
life over to the pestilence; 78:51 And smote all the firstborn in Egypt; the
chief of [their] strength in the tabernacles of Ham: 78:52 But made his own
people to go forth like sheep, and guided them in the wilderness like a flock.
78:53 And he led them on safely, so that they feared not: but the sea
overwhelmed their enemies. 78:54 And he brought them to the border of his
sanctuary, [even to] this mountain, [which] his right hand had purchased.
78:55 He cast out the heathen also before them, and divided them an
inheritance by line, and made the tribes of Israel to dwell in their tents. 78:56
Yet they tempted and provoked the most high God, and kept not his
testimonies: 78:57 But turned back, and dealt unfaithfully like their fathers:
they were turned aside like a deceitful bow. 78:58 For they provoked him to
anger with their high places, and moved him to jealousy with their graven
images. 78:59 When God heard [this], he was wroth, and greatly abhorred
Israel: 78:60 So that he forsook the tabernacle of Shiloh, the tent [which] he
placed among men; 78:61 And delivered his strength into captivity, and his
glory into the enemy's hand. 78:62 He gave his people over also unto the
sword; and was wroth with his inheritance. 78:63 The fire consumed their
young men; and their maidens were not given to marriage. 78:64 Their
priests fell by the sword; and their widows made no lamentation. 78:65 Then
the Lord awaked as one out of sleep, [and] like a mighty man that shouteth
by reason of wine. 78:66 And he smote his enemies in the hinder parts: he
put them to a perpetual reproach. 78:67 Moreover he refused the tabernacle
of Joseph, and chose not the tribe of Ephraim: 78:68 But chose the tribe of
Judah, the mount Zion which he loved. 78:69 And he built his sanctuary like
high [palaces], like the earth which he hath established for ever. 78:70 He
chose David also his servant, and took him from the sheepfolds: 78:71 From
following the ewes great with young he brought him to feed Jacob his people,
and Israel his inheritance. 78:72 So he fed them according to the integrity of
his heart; and guided them by the skilfulness of his hands.

PSALM 79

A PSALM of Asaph. 79:1 O God, the heathen are come into thine inheritance; thy holy temple have they defiled; they have laid Jerusalem on heaps. 79:2 The dead bodies of thy servants have they given [to be] meat unto the fowls of the heaven, the flesh of thy saints unto the beasts of the earth. 79:3 Their blood have they shed like water round about Jerusalem; and [there was] none to bury [them]. 79:4 We are become a reproach to our neighbours, a scorn and derision to them that are round about us. 79:5 How long, LORD? wilt thou be angry for ever? shall thy jealousy burn like fire? 79:6 Pour out thy wrath upon the heathen that have not known thee, and upon the kingdoms that have not called upon thy name. 79:7 For they have devoured Jacob, and laid waste his dwelling place. 79:8 O remember not against us former iniquities: let thy tender mercies speedily prevent us: for we are brought very low. 79:9 Help us, O God of our salvation, for the glory of thy name: and deliver us, and purge away our sins, for thy name's sake. 79:10 Wherefore should the heathen say, Where [is] their God? let him be known among the heathen in our sight [by] the revenging of the blood of thy servants [which is] shed. 79:11 Let the sighing of the prisoner come before thee; according to the greatness of thy power preserve thou those that are appointed to die; 79:12 And render unto our neighbours sevenfold into their bosom their reproach, wherewith they have reproached thee, O Lord. 79:13 So we thy people and sheep of thy pasture will give thee thanks for ever: we will shew forth thy praise to all generations.

PSALM 80

To the chief Musician upon ShoshannimEduth, A PSALM of Asaph. 80:1 Give ear, O Shepherd of Israel, thou that leadest Joseph like a flock; thou that dwellest [between] the cherubims, shine forth. 80:2 Before Ephraim and Benjamin and Manasseh stir up thy strength, and come [and] save us. 80:3 Turn us again, O God, and cause thy face to shine; and we shall be saved. 80:4 O LORD God of hosts, how long wilt thou be angry against the prayer of thy people? 80:5 Thou feedest them with the bread of tears; and givest

them tears to drink in great measure. 80:6 Thou makest us a strife unto our
neighbours: and our enemies laugh among themselves. 80:7 Turn us again,
O God of hosts, and cause thy face to shine; and we shall be saved. 80:8
Thou hast brought a vine out of Egypt: thou hast cast out the heathen, and
planted it. 80:9 Thou preparedst [room] before it, and didst cause it to take
deep root, and it filled the land. 80:10 The hills were covered with the
shadow of it, and the boughs thereof [were like] the goodly cedars. 80:11 She
sent out her boughs unto the sea, and her branches unto the river. 80:12
Why hast thou [then] broken down her hedges, so that all they which pass by
the way do pluck her? 80:13 The boar out of the wood doth waste it, and the
wild beast of the field doth devour it. 80:14 Return, we beseech thee, O God
of hosts: look down from heaven, and behold, and visit this vine; 80:15 And
the vineyard which thy right hand hath planted, and the branch [that] thou
madest strong for thyself. 80:16 [It is] burned with fire, [it is] cut down: they
perish at the rebuke of thy countenance. 80:17 Let thy hand be upon the
man of thy right hand, upon the son of man [whom] thou madest strong for
thyself. 80:18 So will not we go back from thee: quicken us, and we will call
upon thy name. 80:19 Turn us again, O LORD God of hosts, cause thy face
to shine; and we shall be saved.

PSALM 81

To the chief Musician upon Gittith, [A PSALM] of Asaph. 81:1 Sing aloud
unto God our strength: make a joyful noise unto the God of Jacob. 81:2 Take
a PSALM, and bring hither the timbrel, the pleasant harp with the psaltery.
81:3 Blow up the trumpet in the new moon, in the time appointed, on our
solemn feast day. 81:4 For this [was] a statute for Israel, [and] a law of the
God of Jacob. 81:5 This he ordained in Joseph [for] a testimony, when he
went out through the land of Egypt: [where] I heard a language [that] I
understood not. 81:6 I removed his shoulder from the burden: his hands
were delivered from the pots. 81:7 Thou calledst in trouble, and I delivered
thee; I answered thee in the secret place of thunder: I proved thee at the
waters of Meribah. Selah. 81:8 Hear, O my people, and I will testify unto

thee: O Israel, if thou wilt hearken unto me; 81:9 There shall no strange god be in thee; neither shalt thou worship any strange god. 81:10 I [am] the LORD thy God, which brought thee out of the land of Egypt: open thy mouth wide, and I will fill it. 81:11 But my people would not hearken to my voice; and Israel would none of me. 81:12 So I gave them up unto their own hearts' lust: [and] they walked in their own counsels. 81:13 Oh that my people had hearkened unto me, [and] Israel had walked in my ways! 81:14 I should soon have subdued their enemies, and turned my hand against their adversaries. 81:15 The haters of the LORD should have submitted themselves unto him: but their time should have endured for ever. 81:16 He should have fed them also with the finest of the wheat: and with honey out of the rock should I have satisfied thee.

PSALM 82

A PSALM of Asaph. 82:1 God standeth in the congregation of the mighty; he judgeth among the gods. 82:2 How long will ye judge unjustly, and accept the persons of the wicked? Selah. 82:3 Defend the poor and fatherless: do justice to the afflicted and needy. 82:4 Deliver the poor and needy: rid [them] out of the hand of the wicked. 82:5 They know not, neither will they understand; they walk on in darkness: all the foundations of the earth are out of course. 82:6 I have said, Ye [are] gods; and all of you [are] children of the most High. 82:7 But ye shall die like men, and fall like one of the princes. 82:8 Arise, O God, judge the earth: for thou shalt inherit all nations.

PSALM 83

A Song [or] PSALM of Asaph. 83:1 Keep not thou silence, O God: hold not thy peace, and be not still, O God. 83:2 For, lo, thine enemies make a tumult: and they that hate thee have lifted up the head. 83:3 They have taken crafty counsel against thy people, and consulted against thy hidden ones. 83:4 They have said, Come, and let us cut them off from [being] a nation; that the name of Israel may be no more in remembrance. 83:5 For they have consulted together with one consent: they are confederate against thee: 83:6

The tabernacles of Edom, and the Ishmaelites; of Moab, and the Hagarenes;
83:7 Gebal, and Ammon, and Amalek; the Philistines with the inhabitants
of Tyre; 83:8 Assur also is joined with them: they have holpen the children
of Lot. Selah. 83:9 Do unto them as [unto] the Midianites; as [to] Sisera, as
[to] Jabin, at the brook of Kison: 83:10 [Which] perished at Endor: they
became [as] dung for the earth. 83:11 Make their nobles like Oreb, and like
Zeeb: yea, all their princes as Zebah, and as Zalmunna: 83:12 Who said, Let
us take to ourselves the houses of God in possession. 83:13 O my God, make
them like a wheel; as the stubble before the wind. 83:14 As the fire burneth
a wood, and as the flame setteth the mountains on fire; 83:15 So persecute
them with thy tempest, and make them afraid with thy storm. 83:16 Fill their
faces with shame; that they may seek thy name, O LORD. 83:17 Let them be
confounded and troubled for ever; yea, let them be put to shame, and perish:
83:18 That [men] may know that thou, whose name alone [is] JEHOVAH,
[art] the most high over all the earth.

PSALM 84

To the chief Musician upon Gittith, A PSALM for the sons of Korah. 84:1
How amiable [are] thy tabernacles, O LORD of hosts! 84:2 My soul longeth,
yea, even fainteth for the courts of the LORD: my heart and my flesh crieth
out for the living God. 84:3 Yea, the sparrow hath found an house, and the
swallow a nest for herself, where she may lay her young, [even] thine altars,
O LORD of hosts, my King, and my God. 84:4 Blessed [are] they that dwell
in thy house: they will be still praising thee. Selah. 84:5 Blessed [is] the man
whose strength [is] in thee; in whose heart [are] the ways [of them]. 84:6
[Who] passing through the valley of Baca make it a well; the rain also filleth
the pools. 84:7 They go from strength to strength, [every one of them] in
Zion appeareth before God. 84:8 O LORD God of hosts, hear my prayer:
give ear, O God of Jacob. Selah. 84:9 Behold, O God our shield, and look
upon the face of thine anointed. 84:10 For a day in thy courts [is] better than
a thousand. I had rather be a doorkeeper in the house of my God, than to
dwell in the tents of wickedness. 84:11 For the LORD God [is] a sun and

shield: the LORD will give grace and glory: no good [thing] will he withhold from them that walk uprightly. 84:12 O LORD of hosts, blessed [is] the man that trusteth in thee.

PSALM 85

To the chief Musician, A PSALM for the sons of Korah. 85:1 LORD, thou hast been favourable unto thy land: thou hast brought back the captivity of Jacob. 85:2 Thou hast forgiven the iniquity of thy people, thou hast covered all their sin. Selah. 85:3 Thou hast taken away all thy wrath: thou hast turned [thyself] from the fierceness of thine anger. 85:4 Turn us, O God of our salvation, and cause thine anger toward us to cease. 85:5 Wilt thou be angry with us for ever? wilt thou draw out thine anger to all generations? 85:6 Wilt thou not revive us again: that thy people may rejoice in thee? 85:7 Shew us thy mercy, O LORD, and grant us thy salvation. 85:8 I will hear what God the LORD will speak: for he will speak peace unto his people, and to his saints: but let them not turn again to folly. 85:9 Surely his salvation [is] nigh them that fear him; that glory may dwell in our land. 85:10 Mercy and truth are met together; righteousness and peace have kissed [each other]. 85:11 Truth shall spring out of the earth; and righteousness shall look down from heaven. 85:12 Yea, the LORD shall give [that which is] good; and our land shall yield her increase. 85:13 Righteousness shall go before him; and shall set [us] in the way of his steps.

PSALM 86

A Prayer of David. 86:1 Bow down thine ear, O LORD, hear me: for I [am] poor and needy. 86:2 Preserve my soul; for I [am] holy: O thou my God, save thy servant that trusteth in thee. 86:3 Be merciful unto me, O Lord: for I cry unto thee daily. 86:4 Rejoice the soul of thy servant: for unto thee, O Lord, do I lift up my soul. 86:5 For thou, Lord, [art] good, and ready to forgive; and plenteous in mercy unto all them that call upon thee. 86:6 Give ear, O LORD, unto my prayer; and attend to the voice of my supplications. 86:7 In the day of my trouble I will call upon thee: for thou wilt answer me. 86:8

Among the gods [there is] none like unto thee, O Lord; neither [are there any works] like unto thy works. 86:9 All nations whom thou hast made shall come and worship before thee, O Lord; and shall glorify thy name. 86:10 For thou [art] great, and doest wondrous things: thou [art] God alone. 86:11 Teach me thy way, O LORD; I will walk in thy truth: unite my heart to fear thy name. 86:12 I will praise thee, O Lord my God, with all my heart: and I will glorify thy name for evermore. 86:13 For great [is] thy mercy toward me: and thou hast delivered my soul from the lowest hell. 86:14 O God, the proud are risen against me, and the assemblies of violent [men] have sought after my soul; and have not set thee before them. 86:15 But thou, O Lord, [art] a God full of compassion, and gracious, longsuffering, and plenteous in mercy and truth. 86:16 O turn unto me, and have mercy upon me; give thy strength unto thy servant, and save the son of thine handmaid. 86:17 Shew me a token for good; that they which hate me may see [it], and be ashamed: because thou, LORD, hast holpen me, and comforted me.

PSALM 87

A PSALM [or] Song for the sons of Korah. 87:1 His foundation [is] in the holy mountains. 87:2 The LORD loveth the gates of Zion more than all the dwellings of Jacob. 87:3 Glorious things are spoken of thee, O city of God. Selah. 87:4 I will make mention of Rahab and Babylon to them that know me: behold Philistia, and Tyre, with Ethiopia; this [man] was born there. 87:5 And of Zion it shall be said, This and that man was born in her: and the highest himself shall establish her. 87:6 The LORD shall count, when he writeth up the people, [that] this [man] was born there. Selah. 87:7 As well the singers as the players on instruments [shall be there]: all my springs [are] in thee.

PSALM 88

A Song [or] PSALM for the sons of Korah, to the chief Musician upon Mahalath Leannoth, Maschil of Heman the Ezrahite. 88:1 O LORD God of my salvation, I have cried day [and] night before thee: 88:2 Let my prayer

come before thee: incline thine ear unto my cry; 88:3 For my soul is full of
troubles: and my life draweth nigh unto the grave. 88:4 I am counted with
them that go down into the pit: I am as a man [that hath] no strength: 88:5
Free among the dead, like the slain that lie in the grave, whom thou
rememberest no more: and they are cut off from thy hand. 88:6 Thou hast
laid me in the lowest pit, in darkness, in the deeps. 88:7 Thy wrath lieth hard
upon me, and thou hast afflicted [me] with all thy waves. Selah. 88:8 Thou
hast put away mine acquaintance far from me; thou hast made me an
abomination unto them: [I am] shut up, and I cannot come forth. 88:9 Mine
eye mourneth by reason of affliction: LORD, I have called daily upon thee,
I have stretched out my hands unto thee. 88:10 Wilt thou shew wonders to
the dead? shall the dead arise [and] praise thee? Selah. 88:11 Shall thy
lovingkindness be declared in the grave? [or] thy faithfulness in destruction?
88:12 Shall thy wonders be known in the dark? and thy righteousness in the
land of forgetfulness? 88:13 But unto thee have I cried, O LORD; and in the
morning shall my prayer prevent thee. 88:14 LORD, why castest thou off my
soul? [why] hidest thou thy face from me? 88:15 I [am] afflicted and ready to
die from [my] youth up: [while] I suffer thy terrors I am distracted. 88:16 Thy
fierce wrath goeth over me; thy terrors have cut me off. 88:17 They came
round about me daily like water; they compassed me about together. 88:18
Lover and friend hast thou put far from me, [and] mine acquaintance into
darkness.

PSALM 89

Maschil of Ethan the Ezrahite. 89:1 I will sing of the mercies of the LORD
for ever: with my mouth will I make known thy faithfulness to all
generations. 89:2 For I have said, Mercy shall be built up for ever: thy
faithfulness shalt thou establish in the very heavens. 89:3 I have made a
covenant with my chosen, I have sworn unto David my servant, 89:4 Thy
seed will I establish for ever, and build up thy throne to all generations.
Selah. 89:5 And the heavens shall praise thy wonders, O LORD: thy
faithfulness also in the congregation of the saints. 89:6 For who in the

heaven can be compared unto the LORD? [who] among the sons of the
mighty can be likened unto the LORD? 89:7 God is greatly to be feared in
the assembly of the saints, and to be had in reverence of all [them that are]
about him. 89:8 O LORD God of hosts, who [is] a strong LORD like unto
thee? or to thy faithfulness round about thee? 89:9 Thou rulest the raging of
the sea: when the waves thereof arise, thou stillest them. 89:10 Thou hast
broken Rahab in pieces, as one that is slain; thou hast scattered thine
enemies with thy strong arm. 89:11 The heavens [are] thine, the earth also [is]
thine: [as for] the world and the fulness thereof, thou hast founded them.
89:12 The north and the south thou hast created them: Tabor and Hermon
shall rejoice in thy name. 89:13 Thou hast a mighty arm: strong is thy hand,
[and] high is thy right hand. 89:14 Justice and judgment [are] the habitation
of thy throne: mercy and truth shall go before thy face. 89:15 Blessed [is] the
people that know the joyful sound: they shall walk, O LORD, in the light of
thy countenance. 89:16 In thy name shall they rejoice all the day: and in thy
righteousness shall they be exalted. 89:17 For thou [art] the glory of their
strength: and in thy favour our horn shall be exalted. 89:18 For the LORD
[is] our defence; and the Holy One of Israel [is] our king. 89:19 Then thou
spakest in vision to thy holy one, and saidst, I have laid help upon [one that
is] mighty; I have exalted [one] chosen out of the people. 89:20 I have found
David my servant; with my holy oil have I anointed him: 89:21 With whom
my hand shall be established: mine arm also shall strengthen him. 89:22 The
enemy shall not exact upon him; nor the son of wickedness afflict him. 89:23
And I will beat down his foes before his face, and plague them that hate him.
89:24 But my faithfulness and my mercy [shall be] with him: and in my name
shall his horn be exalted. 89:25 I will set his hand also in the sea, and his
right hand in the rivers. 89:26 He shall cry unto me, Thou [art] my father, my
God, and the rock of my salvation. 89:27 Also I will make him [my] firstborn,
higher than the kings of the earth. 89:28 My mercy will I keep for him for
evermore, and my covenant shall stand fast with him. 89:29 His seed also will
I make [to endure] for ever, and his throne as the days of heaven. 89:30 If his
children forsake my law, and walk not in my judgments; 89:31 If they break

my statutes, and keep not my commandments; 89:32 Then will I visit their
transgression with the rod, and their iniquity with stripes. 89:33 Nevertheless
my lovingkindness will I not utterly take from him, nor suffer my faithfulness
to fail. 89:34 My covenant will I not break, nor alter the thing that is gone
out of my lips. 89:35 Once have I sworn by my holiness that I will not lie
unto David. 89:36 His seed shall endure for ever, and his throne as the sun
before me. 89:37 It shall be established for ever as the moon, and [as] a
faithful witness in heaven. Selah. 89:38 But thou hast cast off and abhorred,
thou hast been wroth with thine anointed. 89:39 Thou hast made void the
covenant of thy servant: thou hast profaned his crown [by casting it] to the
ground. 89:40 Thou hast broken down all his hedges; thou hast brought his
strong holds to ruin. 89:41 All that pass by the way spoil him: he is a
reproach to his neighbours. 89:42 Thou hast set up the right hand of his
adversaries; thou hast made all his enemies to rejoice. 89:43 Thou hast also
turned the edge of his sword, and hast not made him to stand in the battle.
89:44 Thou hast made his glory to cease, and cast his throne down to the
ground. 89:45 The days of his youth hast thou shortened: thou hast covered
him with shame. Selah. 89:46 How long, LORD? wilt thou hide thyself for
ever? shall thy wrath burn like fire? 89:47 Remember how short my time is:
wherefore hast thou made all men in vain? 89:48 What man [is he that]
liveth, and shall not see death? shall he deliver his soul from the hand of the
grave? Selah. 89:49 Lord, where [are] thy former lovingkindnesses, [which]
thou swarest unto David in thy truth? 89:50 Remember, Lord, the reproach
of thy servants; [how] I do bear in my bosom [the reproach of] all the mighty
people; 89:51 Wherewith thine enemies have reproached, O LORD;
wherewith they have reproached the footsteof thine anointed. 89:52 Blessed
[be] the LORD for evermore. Amen, and Amen.

PSALM 90

A Prayer of Moses the man of God. 90:1 Lord, thou hast been our dwelling
place in all generations. 90:2 Before the mountains were brought forth, or
ever thou hadst formed the earth and the world, even from everlasting to

everlasting, thou [art] God. 90:3 Thou turnest man to destruction; and sayest,
Return, ye children of men. 90:4 For a thousand years in thy sight [are but]
as yesterday when it is past, and [as] a watch in the night. 90:5 Thou carriest
them away as with a flood; they are [as] a sleep: in the morning [they are] like
grass [which] groweth up. 90:6 In the morning it flourisheth, and groweth up;
in the evening it is cut down, and withereth. 90:7 For we are consumed by
thine anger, and by thy wrath are we troubled. 90:8 Thou hast set our
iniquities before thee, our secret [sins] in the light of thy countenance. 90:9
For all our days are passed away in thy wrath: we spend our years as a tale
[that is told]. 90:10 The days of our years [are] threescore years and ten; and
if by reason of strength [they be] fourscore years, yet [is] their strength labour
and sorrow; for it is soon cut off, and we fly away. 90:11 Who knoweth the
power of thine anger? even according to thy fear, [so is] thy wrath. 90:12 So
teach [us] to number our days, that we may apply [our] hearts unto wisdom.
90:13 Return, O LORD, how long? and let it repent thee concerning thy
servants. 90:14 O satisfy us early with thy mercy; that we may rejoice and be
glad all our days. 90:15 Make us glad according to the days [wherein] thou
hast afflicted us, [and] the years [wherein] we have seen evil. 90:16 Let thy
work appear unto thy servants, and thy glory unto their children. 90:17 And
let the beauty of the LORD our God be upon us: and establish thou the work
of our hands upon us; yea, the work of our hands establish thou it.

PSALM 91

91:1 He that dwelleth in the secret place of the most High shall abide under
the shadow of the Almighty. 91:2 I will say of the LORD, [He is] my refuge
and my fortress: my God; in him will I trust. 91:3 Surely he shall deliver thee
from the snare of the fowler, [and] from the noisome pestilence. 91:4 He
shall cover thee with his feathers, and under his wings shalt thou trust: his
truth [shall be thy] shield and buckler. 91:5 Thou shalt not be afraid for the
terror by night; [nor] for the arrow [that] flieth by day; 91:6 [Nor] for the
pestilence [that] walketh in darkness; [nor] for the destruction [that] wasteth
at noonday. 91:7 A thousand shall fall at thy side, and ten thousand at thy

right hand; [but] it shall not come nigh thee. 91:8 Only with thine eyes shalt thou behold and see the reward of the wicked. 91:9 Because thou hast made the LORD, [which is] my refuge, [even] the most High, thy habitation; 91:10 There shall no evil befall thee, neither shall any plague come nigh thy dwelling. 91:11 For he shall give his angels charge over thee, to keep thee in all thy ways. 91:12 They shall bear thee up in [their] hands, lest thou dash thy foot against a stone. 91:13 Thou shalt tread upon the lion and adder: the young lion and the dragon shalt thou trample under feet. 91:14 Because he hath set his love upon me, therefore will I deliver him: I will set him on high, because he hath known my name. 91:15 He shall call upon me, and I will answer him: I [will be] with him in trouble; I will deliver him, and honour him. 91:16 With long life will I satisfy him, and shew him my salvation.

PSALM 92

A PSALM [or] Song for the sabbath day. 92:1 [It is a] good [thing] to give thanks unto the LORD, and to sing praises unto thy name, O most High: 92:2 To shew forth thy lovingkindness in the morning, and thy faithfulness every night, 92:3 Upon an instrument of ten strings, and upon the psaltery; upon the harp with a solemn sound. 92:4 For thou, LORD, hast made me glad through thy work: I will triumph in the works of thy hands. 92:5 O LORD, how great are thy works! [and] thy thoughts are very deep. 92:6 A brutish man knoweth not; neither doth a fool understand this. 92:7 When the wicked spring as the grass, and when all the workers of iniquity do flourish; [it is] that they shall be destroyed for ever: 92:8 But thou, LORD, [art most] high for evermore. 92:9 For, lo, thine enemies, O LORD, for, lo, thine enemies shall perish; all the workers of iniquity shall be scattered. 92:10 But my horn shalt thou exalt like [the horn of] an unicorn: I shall be anointed with fresh oil. 92:11 Mine eye also shall see [my desire] on mine enemies, [and] mine ears shall hear [my desire] of the wicked that rise up against me. 92:12 The righteous shall flourish like the palm tree: he shall grow like a cedar in Lebanon. 92:13 Those that be planted in the house of the LORD shall flourish in the courts of our God. 92:14 They shall still bring

forth fruit in old age; they shall be fat and flourishing; 92:15 To shew that the
LORD [is] upright: [he is] my rock, and [there is] no unrighteousness in him.

PSALM 93
93:1 The LORD reigneth, he is clothed with majesty; the LORD is clothed
with strength, [wherewith] he hath girded himself: the world also is
stablished, that it cannot be moved. 93:2 Thy throne [is] established of old:
thou [art] from everlasting. 93:3 The floods have lifted up, O LORD, the
floods have lifted up their voice; the floods lift up their waves. 93:4 The
LORD on high [is] mightier than the noise of many waters, [yea, than] the
mighty waves of the sea. 93:5 Thy testimonies are very sure: holiness
becometh thine house, O LORD, for ever.

PSALM 94
94:1 O LORD God, to whom vengeance belongeth; O God, to whom
vengeance belongeth, shew thyself. 94:2 Lift up thyself, thou judge of the
earth: render a reward to the proud. 94:3 LORD, how long shall the wicked,
how long shall the wicked triumph? 94:4 [How long] shall they utter [and]
speak hard things? [and] all the workers of iniquity boast themselves? 94:5
They break in pieces thy people, O LORD, and afflict thine heritage. 94:6
They slay the widow and the stranger, and murder the fatherless. 94:7 Yet
they say, The LORD shall not see, neither shall the God of Jacob regard [it].
94:8 Understand, ye brutish among the people: and [ye] fools, when will ye
be wise? 94:9 He that planted the ear, shall he not hear? he that formed the
eye, shall he not see? 94:10 He that chastiseth the heathen, shall not he
correct? he that teacheth man knowledge, [shall not he know]? 94:11 The
LORD knoweth the thoughts of man, that they [are] vanity. 94:12 Blessed [is]
the man whom thou chastenest, O LORD, and teachest him out of thy law;
94:13 That thou mayest give him rest from the days of adversity, until the pit
be digged for the wicked. 94:14 For the LORD will not cast off his people,
neither will he forsake his inheritance. 94:15 But judgment shall return unto
righteousness: and all the upright in heart shall follow it. 94:16 Who will rise

up for me against the evildoers? [or] who will stand up for me against the workers of iniquity? 94:17 Unless the LORD [had been] my help, my soul had almost dwelt in silence. 94:18 When I said, My foot slippeth; thy mercy, O LORD, held me up. 94:19 In the multitude of my thoughts within me thy comforts delight my soul. 94:20 Shall the throne of iniquity have fellowship with thee, which frameth mischief by a law? 94:21 They gather themselves together against the soul of the righteous, and condemn the innocent blood. 94:22 But the LORD is my defence; and my God [is] the rock of my refuge. 94:23 And he shall bring upon them their own iniquity, and shall cut them off in their own wickedness; [yea], the LORD our God shall cut them off.

PSALM 95

95:1 O come, let us sing unto the LORD: let us make a joyful noise to the rock of our salvation. 95:2 Let us come before his presence with thanksgiving, and make a joyful noise unto him with PSALMs. 95:3 For the LORD [is] a great God, and a great King above all gods. 95:4 In his hand [are] the deep places of the earth: the strength of the hills [is] his also. 95:5 The sea [is] his, and he made it: and his hands formed the dry [land]. 95:6 O come, let us worship and bow down: let us kneel before the LORD our maker. 95:7 For he [is] our God; and we [are] the people of his pasture, and the sheep of his hand. To day if ye will hear his voice, 95:8 Harden not your heart, as in the provocation, [and] as [in] the day of temptation in the wilderness: 95:9 When your fathers tempted me, proved me, and saw my work. 95:10 Forty years long was I grieved with [this] generation, and said, It [is] a people that do err in their heart, and they have not known my ways: 95:11 Unto whom I sware in my wrath that they should not enter into my rest.

PSALM 96

96:1 O sing unto the LORD a new song: sing unto the LORD, all the earth. 96:2 Sing unto the LORD, bless his name; shew forth his salvation from day to day. 96:3 Declare his glory among the heathen, his wonders among all people. 96:4 For the LORD [is] great, and greatly to be praised: he [is] to be feared above all gods. 96:5 For all the gods of the nations [are] idols: but the LORD made the heavens. 96:6 Honour and majesty [are] before him: strength and beauty [are] in his sanctuary. 96:7 Give unto the LORD, O ye kindreds of the people, give unto the LORD glory and strength. 96:8 Give unto the LORD the glory [due unto] his name: bring an offering, and come into his courts. 96:9 O worship the LORD in the beauty of holiness: fear before him, all the earth. 96:10 Say among the heathen [that] the LORD reigneth: the world also shall be established that it shall not be moved: he shall judge the people righteously. 96:11 Let the heavens rejoice, and let the earth be glad; let the sea roar, and the fulness thereof. 96:12 Let the field be joyful, and all that [is] therein: then shall all the trees of the wood rejoice 96:13 Before the LORD: for he cometh, for he cometh to judge the earth: he shall judge the world with righteousness, and the people with his truth.

PSALM 97

97:1 The LORD reigneth; let the earth rejoice; let the multitude of isles be glad [thereof]. 97:2 Clouds and darkness [are] round about him: righteousness and judgment [are] the habitation of his throne. 97:3 A fire goeth before him, and burneth up his enemies round about. 97:4 His lightnings enlightened the world: the earth saw, and trembled. 97:5 The hills melted like wax at the presence of the LORD, at the presence of the Lord of the whole earth. 97:6 The heavens declare his righteousness, and all the people see his glory. 97:7 Confounded be all they that serve graven images, that boast themselves of idols: worship him, all [ye] gods. 97:8 Zion heard, and was glad; and the daughters of Judah rejoiced because of thy judgments, O LORD. 97:9 For thou, LORD, [art] high above all the earth: thou art exalted far above all gods. 97:10 Ye that love the LORD, hate evil: he preserveth the souls of his saints; he delivereth them out of the hand of the wicked. 97:11 Light is sown for the righteous, and gladness for the upright in heart. 97:12 Rejoice in the LORD, ye righteous; and give thanks at the remembrance of his holiness.

PSALM 98

A PSALM. 98:1 O sing unto the LORD a new song; for he hath done marvellous things: his right hand, and his holy arm, hath gotten him the victory. 98:2 The LORD hath made known his salvation: his righteousness hath he openly shewed in the sight of the heathen. 98:3 He hath remembered his mercy and his truth toward the house of Israel: all the ends of the earth have seen the salvation of our God. 98:4 Make a joyful noise unto the LORD, all the earth: make a loud noise, and rejoice, and sing praise. 98:5 Sing unto the LORD with the harp; with the harp, and the voice of a PSALM. 98:6 With trumpets and sound of cornet make a joyful noise before the LORD, the King. 98:7 Let the sea roar, and the fulness thereof; the world, and they that dwell therein. 98:8 Let the floods clap [their] hands: let the hills be joyful together 98:9 Before the LORD; for he cometh to judge the earth: with righteousness shall he judge the world, and the people with equity.

PSALM 99

99:1 The LORD reigneth; let the people tremble: he sitteth [between] the cherubims; let the earth be moved. 99:2 The LORD [is] great in Zion; and he [is] high above all the people. 99:3 Let them praise thy great and terrible name; [for] it [is] holy. 99:4 The king's strength also loveth judgment; thou dost establish equity, thou executest judgment and righteousness in Jacob. 99:5 Exalt ye the LORD our God, and worship at his footstool; [for] he [is] holy. 99:6 Moses and Aaron among his priests, and Samuel among them that call upon his name; they called upon the LORD, and he answered them. 99:7 He spake unto them in the cloudy pillar: they kept his testimonies, and the ordinance [that] he gave them. 99:8 Thou answeredst them, O LORD our God: thou wast a God that forgavest them, though thou tookest vengeance of their inventions. 99:9 Exalt the LORD our God, and worship at his holy hill; for the LORD our God [is] holy.

PSALM 100

A PSALM of praise. 100:1 Make a joyful noise unto the LORD, all ye lands. 100:2 Serve the LORD with gladness: come before his presence with singing. 100:3 Know ye that the LORD he [is] God: [it is] he [that] hath made us, and not we ourselves; [we are] his people, and the sheep of his pasture. 100:4 Enter into his gates with thanksgiving, [and] into his courts with praise: be thankful unto him, [and] bless his name. 100:5 For the LORD [is] good; his mercy [is] everlasting; and his truth [endureth] to all generations.

PSALM 101

A PSALM of David. 101:1 I will sing of mercy and judgment: unto thee, O LORD, will I sing. 101:2 I will behave myself wisely in a perfect way. O when wilt thou come unto me? I will walk within my house with a perfect heart. 101:3 I will set no wicked thing before mine eyes: I hate the work of them that turn aside; [it] shall not cleave to me. 101:4 A froward heart shall depart from me: I will not know a wicked [person]. 101:5 Whoso privily slandereth his neighbour, him will I cut off: him that hath an high look and a proud heart will not I suffer. 101:6 Mine eyes [shall be] upon the faithful of the land, that they may dwell with me: he that walketh in a perfect way, he shall serve me. 101:7 He that worketh deceit shall not dwell within my house: he that telleth lies shall not tarry in my sight. 101:8 I will early destroy all the wicked of the land; that I may cut off all wicked doers from the city of the LORD.

PSALM 102

A Prayer of the afflicted, when he is overwhelmed, and poureth out his complaint before the LORD. 102:1 Hear my prayer, O LORD, and let my cry come unto thee. 102:2 Hide not thy face from me in the day [when] I am in trouble; incline thine ear unto me: in the day [when] I call answer me speedily. 102:3 For my days are consumed like smoke, and my bones are burned as an hearth. 102:4 My heart is smitten, and withered like grass; so that I forget to eat my bread. 102:5 By reason of the voice of my groaning my bones cleave to my skin. 102:6 I am like a pelican of the wilderness: I am like an owl of the desert. 102:7 I watch, and am as a sparrow alone upon the house top. 102:8 Mine enemies reproach me all the day; [and] they that are mad against me are sworn against me. 102:9 For I have eaten ashes like bread, and mingled my drink with weeping, 102:10 Because of thine indignation and thy wrath: for thou hast lifted me up, and cast me down. 102:11 My days [are] like a shadow that declineth; and I am withered like grass. 102:12 But thou, O LORD, shalt endure for ever; and thy remembrance unto all generations. 102:13 Thou shalt arise, [and] have mercy upon Zion: for the time to favour her, yea, the set time, is come. 102:14 For thy servants take pleasure in her stones, and favour the dust thereof. 102:15 So the heathen shall fear the name of the LORD, and all the kings of the earth thy glory. 102:16 When the LORD shall build up Zion, he shall appear in his glory. 102:17 He will regard the prayer of the destitute, and not despise their prayer. 102:18 This shall be written for the generation to come: and the people which shall be created shall praise the LORD. 102:19 For he hath looked down from the height of his sanctuary; from heaven did the LORD behold the earth; 102:20 To hear the groaning of the prisoner; to loose those that are appointed to death; 102:21 To declare the name of the LORD in Zion, and his praise in Jerusalem; 102:22 When the people are gathered together, and the kingdoms, to serve the LORD. 102:23 He weakened my strength in the way; he shortened my days. 102:24 I said, O my God, take me not away in the midst of my days: thy years [are] throughout all generations. 102:25 Of old hast thou laid the foundation of the earth: and the heavens [are] the work of thy hands. 102:26 They shall perish, but thou shalt endure: yea, all of them shall wax old like a garment; as a vesture shalt thou change them, and they shall be changed: 102:27 But thou [art] the same, and thy years shall have no end. 102:28 The children of thy servants shall continue, and their seed shall be established before thee.

PSALM 103

[A PSALM] of David. 103:1 Bless the LORD, O my soul: and all that is

within me, [bless] his holy name. 103:2 Bless the LORD, O my soul, and
forget not all his benefits: 103:3 Who forgiveth all thine iniquities; who
healeth all thy diseases; 103:4 Who redeemeth thy life from destruction; who
crowneth thee with lovingkindness and tender mercies; 103:5 Who satisfieth
thy mouth with good [things; so that] thy youth is renewed like the eagle's.
103:6 The LORD executeth righteousness and judgment for all that are
oppressed. 103:7 He made known his ways unto Moses, his acts unto the
children of Israel. 103:8 The LORD [is] merciful and gracious, slow to anger,
and plenteous in mercy. 103:9 He will not always chide: neither will he keep
[his anger] for ever. 103:10 He hath not dealt with us after our sins; nor
rewarded us according to our iniquities. 103:11 For as the heaven is high
above the earth, [so] great is his mercy toward them that fear him. 103:12 As
far as the east is from the west, [so] far hath he removed our transgressions
from us. 103:13 Like as a father pitieth [his] children, [so] the LORD pitieth
them that fear him. 103:14 For he knoweth our frame; he remembereth that
we [are] dust. 103:15 [As for] man, his days [are] as grass: as a flower of the
field, so he flourisheth. 103:16 For the wind passeth over it, and it is gone;
and the place thereof shall know it no more. 103:17 But the mercy of the
LORD [is] from everlasting to everlasting upon them that fear him, and his
righteousness unto children's children; 103:18 To such as keep his covenant,
and to those that remember his commandments to do them. 103:19 The
LORD hath prepared his throne in the heavens; and his kingdom ruleth over
all. 103:20 Bless the LORD, ye his angels, that excel in strength, that do his
commandments, hearkening unto the voice of his word. 103:21 Bless ye the
LORD, all [ye] his hosts; [ye] ministers of his, that do his pleasure. 103:22
Bless the LORD, all his works in all places of his dominion: bless the LORD,
O my soul.

PSALM 104

104:1 Bless the LORD, O my soul. O LORD my God, thou art very great;
thou art clothed with honour and majesty. 104:2 Who coverest [thyself] with
light as [with] a garment: who stretchest out the heavens like a curtain: 104:3

Who layeth the beams of his chambers in the waters: who maketh the clouds his chariot: who walketh upon the wings of the wind: 104:4 Who maketh his angels spirits; his ministers a flaming fire: 104:5 [Who] laid the foundations of the earth, [that] it should not be removed for ever. 104:6 Thou coveredst it with the deep as [with] a garment: the waters stood above the mountains. 104:7 At thy rebuke they fled; at the voice of thy thunder they hasted away. 104:8 They go up by the mountains; they go down by the valleys unto the place which thou hast founded for them. 104:9 Thou hast set a bound that they may not pass over; that they turn not again to cover the earth. 104:10 He sendeth the springs into the valleys, [which] run among the hills. 104:11 They give drink to every beast of the field: the wild asses quench their thirst. 104:12 By them shall the fowls of the heaven have their habitation, [which] sing among the branches. 104:13 He watereth the hills from his chambers: the earth is satisfied with the fruit of thy works. 104:14 He causeth the grass to grow for the cattle, and herb for the service of man: that he may bring forth food out of the earth; 104:15 And wine [that] maketh glad the heart of man, [and] oil to make [his] face to shine, and bread [which] strengtheneth man's heart. 104:16 The trees of the LORD are full [of sap]; the cedars of Lebanon, which he hath planted; 104:17 Where the birds make their nests: [as for] the stork, the fir trees [are] her house. 104:18 The high hills [are] a refuge for the wild goats; [and] the rocks for the conies. 104:19 He appointed the moon for seasons: the sun knoweth his going down. 104:20 Thou makest darkness, and it is night: wherein all the beasts of the forest do creep [forth]. 104:21 The young lions roar after their prey, and seek their meat from God. 104:22 The sun ariseth, they gather themselves together, and lay them down in their dens. 104:23 Man goeth forth unto his work and to his labour until the evening. 104:24 O LORD, how manifold are thy works! in wisdom hast thou made them all: the earth is full of thy riches. 104:25 [So is] this great and wide sea, wherein [are] things creeping innumerable, both small and great beasts. 104:26 There go the ships: [there is] that leviathan, [whom] thou hast made to play therein. 104:27 These wait all upon thee; that thou mayest give [them] their meat in due season. 104:28 [That] thou givest them they

gather: thou openest thine hand, they are filled with good. 104:29 Thou
hidest thy face, they are troubled: thou takest away their breath, they die, and
return to their dust. 104:30 Thou sendest forth thy spirit, they are created:
and thou renewest the face of the earth. 104:31 The glory of the LORD shall
endure for ever: the LORD shall rejoice in his works. 104:32 He looketh on
the earth, and it trembleth: he toucheth the hills, and they smoke. 104:33 I
will sing unto the LORD as long as I live: I will sing praise to my God while
I have my being. 104:34 My meditation of him shall be sweet: I will be glad
in the LORD. 104:35 Let the sinners be consumed out of the earth, and let
the wicked be no more. Bless thou the LORD, O my soul. Praise ye the
LORD.

PSALM 105

105:1 O give thanks unto the LORD; call upon his name: make known his
deeds among the people. 105:2 Sing unto him, sing PSALMs unto him: talk
ye of all his wondrous works. 105:3 Glory ye in his holy name: let the heart
of them rejoice that seek the LORD. 105:4 Seek the LORD, and his strength:
seek his face evermore. 105:5 Remember his marvellous works that he hath
done; his wonders, and the judgments of his mouth; 105:6 O ye seed of
Abraham his servant, ye children of Jacob his chosen. 105:7 He [is] the
LORD our God: his judgments [are] in all the earth. 105:8 He hath
remembered his covenant for ever, the word [which] he commanded to a
thousand generations. 105:9 Which [covenant] he made with Abraham, and
his oath unto Isaac; 105:10 And confirmed the same unto Jacob for a law,
[and] to Israel [for] an everlasting covenant: 105:11 Saying, Unto thee will I
give the land of Canaan, the lot of your inheritance: 105:12 When they were
[but] a few men in number; yea, very few, and strangers in it. 105:13 When
they went from one nation to another, from [one] kingdom to another
people; 105:14 He suffered no man to do them wrong: yea, he reproved kings
for their sakes; 105:15 [Saying], Touch not mine anointed, and do my
prophets no harm. 105:16 Moreover he called for a famine upon the land:
he brake the whole staff of bread. 105:17 He sent a man before them, [even]

Joseph, [who] was sold for a servant: 105:18 Whose feet they hurt with fetters: he was laid in iron: 105:19 Until the time that his word came: the word of the LORD tried him. 105:20 The king sent and loosed him; [even] the ruler of the people, and let him go free. 105:21 He made him lord of his house, and ruler of all his substance: 105:22 To bind his princes at his pleasure; and teach his senators wisdom. 105:23 Israel also came into Egypt; and Jacob sojourned in the land of Ham. 105:24 And he increased his people greatly; and made them stronger than their enemies. 105:25 He turned their heart to hate his people, to deal subtilly with his servants. 105:26 He sent Moses his servant; [and] Aaron whom he had chosen. 105:27 They shewed his signs among them, and wonders in the land of Ham. 105:28 He sent darkness, and made it dark; and they rebelled not against his word. 105:29 He turned their waters into blood, and slew their fish. 105:30 Their land brought forth frogs in abundance, in the chambers of their kings. 105:31 He spake, and there came divers sorts of flies, [and] lice in all their coasts. 105:32 He gave them hail for rain, [and] flaming fire in their land. 105:33 He smote their vines also and their fig trees; and brake the trees of their coasts. 105:34 He spake, and the locusts came, and caterpillers, and that without number, 105:35 And did eat up all the herbs in their land, and devoured the fruit of their ground. 105:36 He smote also all the firstborn in their land, the chief of all their strength. 105:37 He brought them forth also with silver and gold: and [there was] not one feeble [person] among their tribes. 105:38 Egypt was glad when they departed: for the fear of them fell upon them. 105:39 He spread a cloud for a covering; and fire to give light in the night. 105:40 [The people] asked, and he brought quails, and satisfied them with the bread of heaven. 105:41 He opened the rock, and the waters gushed out; they ran in the dry places [like] a river. 105:42 For he remembered his holy promise, [and] Abraham his servant. 105:43 And he brought forth his people with joy, [and] his chosen with gladness: 105:44 And gave them the lands of the heathen: and they inherited the labour of the people; 105:45 That they might observe his statutes, and keep his laws. Praise ye the LORD.

PSALMS

PSALM 106

106:1 Praise ye the LORD. O give thanks unto the LORD; for [he is] good:
for his mercy [endureth] for ever. 106:2 Who can utter the mighty acts of the
LORD? [who] can shew forth all his praise? 106:3 Blessed [are] they that keep
judgment, [and] he that doeth righteousness at all times. 106:4 Remember
me, O LORD, with the favour [that thou bearest unto] thy people: O visit me
with thy salvation; 106:5 That I may see the good of thy chosen, that I may
rejoice in the gladness of thy nation, that I may glory with thine inheritance.
106:6 We have sinned with our fathers, we have committed iniquity, we have
done wickedly. 106:7 Our fathers understood not thy wonders in Egypt; they
remembered not the multitude of thy mercies; but provoked [him] at the sea,
[even] at the Red sea. 106:8 Nevertheless he saved them for his name's sake,
that he might make his mighty power to be known. 106:9 He rebuked the
Red sea also, and it was dried up: so he led them through the depths, as
through the wilderness. 106:10 And he saved them from the hand of him
that hated [them], and redeemed them from the hand of the enemy. 106:11
And the waters covered their enemies: there was not one of them left. 106:12
Then believed they his words; they sang his praise. 106:13 They soon forgat
his works; they waited not for his counsel: 106:14 But lusted exceedingly in
the wilderness, and tempted God in the desert. 106:15 And he gave them
their request; but sent leanness into their soul. 106:16 They envied Moses
also in the camp, [and] Aaron the saint of the LORD. 106:17 The earth
opened and swallowed up Dathan, and covered the company of Abiram.
106:18 And a fire was kindled in their company; the flame burned up the
wicked. 106:19 They made a calf in Horeb, and worshipped the molten
image. 106:20 Thus they changed their glory into the similitude of an ox that
eateth grass. 106:21 They forgat God their saviour, which had done great
things in Egypt; 106:22 Wondrous works in the land of Ham, [and] terrible
things by the Red sea. 106:23 Therefore he said that he would destroy them,
had not Moses his chosen stood before him in the breach, to turn away his
wrath, lest he should destroy [them]. 106:24 Yea, they despised the pleasant
land, they believed not his word: 106:25 But murmured in their tents, [and]

hearkened not unto the voice of the LORD. 106:26 Therefore he lifted up his hand against them, to overthrow them in the wilderness: 106:27 To overthrow their seed also among the nations, and to scatter them in the lands. 106:28 They joined themselves also unto Baalpeor, and ate the sacrifices of the dead. 106:29 Thus they provoked [him] to anger with their inventions: and the plague brake in upon them. 106:30 Then stood up Phinehas, and executed judgment: and [so] the plague was stayed. 106:31 And that was counted unto him for righteousness unto all generations for evermore. 106:32 They angered [him] also at the waters of strife, so that it went ill with Moses for their sakes: 106:33 Because they provoked his spirit, so that he spake unadvisedly with his lips. 106:34 They did not destroy the nations, concerning whom the LORD commanded them: 106:35 But were mingled among the heathen, and learned their works. 106:36 And they served their idols: which were a snare unto them. 106:37 Yea, they sacrificed their sons and their daughters unto devils, 106:38 And shed innocent blood, [even] the blood of their sons and of their daughters, whom they sacrificed unto the idols of Canaan: and the land was polluted with blood. 106:39 Thus were they defiled with their own works, and went a whoring with their own inventions. 106:40 Therefore was the wrath of the LORD kindled against his people, insomuch that he abhorred his own inheritance. 106:41 And he gave them into the hand of the heathen; and they that hated them ruled over them. 106:42 Their enemies also oppressed them, and they were brought into subjection under their hand. 106:43 Many times did he deliver them; but they provoked [him] with their counsel, and were brought low for their iniquity. 106:44 Nevertheless he regarded their affliction, when he heard their cry: 106:45 And he remembered for them his covenant, and repented according to the multitude of his mercies. 106:46 He made them also to be pitied of all those that carried them captives. 106:47 Save us, O LORD our God, and gather us from among the heathen, to give thanks unto thy holy name, [and] to triumph in thy praise. 106:48 Blessed [be] the LORD God of Israel from everlasting to everlasting: and let all the people say, Amen. Praise ye the LORD.

PSALMS

PSALM 107
107:1 O give thanks unto the LORD, for [he is] good: for his mercy
[endureth] for ever. 107:2 Let the redeemed of the LORD say [so], whom he
hath redeemed from the hand of the enemy; 107:3 And gathered them out
of the lands, from the east, and from the west, from the north, and from the
south. 107:4 They wandered in the wilderness in a solitary way; they found
no city to dwell in. 107:5 Hungry and thirsty, their soul fainted in them.
107:6 Then they cried unto the LORD in their trouble, [and] he delivered
them out of their distresses. 107:7 And he led them forth by the right way,
that they might go to a city of habitation. 107:8 Oh that [men] would praise
the LORD [for] his goodness, and [for] his wonderful works to the children
of men! 107:9 For he satisfieth the longing soul, and filleth the hungry soul
with goodness. 107:10 Such as sit in darkness and in the shadow of death,
[being] bound in affliction and iron; 107:11 Because they rebelled against the
words of God, and contemned the counsel of the most High: 107:12
Therefore he brought down their heart with labour; they fell down, and
[there was] none to help. 107:13 Then they cried unto the LORD in their
trouble, [and] he saved them out of their distresses. 107:14 He brought them
out of darkness and the shadow of death, and brake their bands in sunder.
107:15 Oh that [men] would praise the LORD [for] his goodness, and [for]
his wonderful works to the children of men! 107:16 For he hath broken the
gates of brass, and cut the bars of iron in sunder. 107:17 Fools because of
their transgression, and because of their iniquities, are afflicted. 107:18 Their
soul abhorreth all manner of meat; and they draw near unto the gates of
death. 107:19 Then they cry unto the LORD in their trouble, [and] he saveth
them out of their distresses. 107:20 He sent his word, and healed them, and
delivered [them] from their destructions. 107:21 Oh that [men] would praise
the LORD [for] his goodness, and [for] his wonderful works to the children
of men! 107:22 And let them sacrifice the sacrifices of thanksgiving, and
declare his works with rejoicing. 107:23 They that go down to the sea in
ships, that do business in great waters; 107:24 These see the works of the
LORD, and his wonders in the deep. 107:25 For he commandeth, and

raiseth the stormy wind, which lifteth up the waves thereof. 107:26 They
mount up to the heaven, they go down again to the depths: their soul is
melted because of trouble. 107:27 They reel to and fro, and stagger like a
drunken man, and are at their wits' end. 107:28 Then they cry unto the
LORD in their trouble, and he bringeth them out of their distresses. 107:29
He maketh the storm a calm, so that the waves thereof are still. 107:30 Then
are they glad because they be quiet; so he bringeth them unto their desired
haven. 107:31 Oh that [men] would praise the LORD [for] his goodness, and
[for] his wonderful works to the children of men! 107:32 Let them exalt him
also in the congregation of the people, and praise him in the assembly of the
elders. 107:33 He turneth rivers into a wilderness, and the watersprings into
dry ground; 107:34 A fruitful land into barrenness, for the wickedness of
them that dwell therein. 107:35 He turneth the wilderness into a standing
water, and dry ground into watersprings. 107:36 And there he maketh the
hungry to dwell, that they may prepare a city for habitation; 107:37 And sow
the fields, and plant vineyards, which may yield fruits of increase. 107:38 He
blesseth them also, so that they are multiplied greatly; and suffereth not their
cattle to decrease. 107:39 Again, they are minished and brought low through
oppression, affliction, and sorrow. 107:40 He poureth contempt upon
princes, and causeth them to wander in the wilderness, [where there is] no
way. 107:41 Yet setteth he the poor on high from affliction, and maketh
[him] families like a flock. 107:42 The righteous shall see [it], and rejoice: and
all iniquity shall stop her mouth. 107:43 Whoso [is] wise, and will observe
these [things], even they shall understand the lovingkindness of the LORD.

PSALM 108

A Song [or] PSALM of David. 108:1 O God, my heart is fixed; I will sing and
give praise, even with my glory. 108:2 Awake, psaltery and harp: I [myself] will
awake early. 108:3 I will praise thee, O LORD, among the people: and I will
sing praises unto thee among the nations. 108:4 For thy mercy [is] great
above the heavens: and thy truth [reacheth] unto the clouds. 108:5 Be thou
exalted, O God, above the heavens: and thy glory above all the earth; 108:6

That thy beloved may be delivered: save [with] thy right hand, and answer
me. 108:7 God hath spoken in his holiness; I will rejoice, I will divide
Shechem, and mete out the valley of Succoth. 108:8 Gilead [is] mine;
Manasseh [is] mine; Ephraim also [is] the strength of mine head; Judah [is]
my lawgiver; 108:9 Moab [is] my washpot; over Edom will I cast out my shoe;
over Philistia will I triumph. 108:10 Who will bring me into the strong city?
who will lead me into Edom? 108:11 [Wilt] not [thou], O God, [who] hast
cast us off? and wilt not thou, O God, go forth with our hosts? 108:12 Give
us help from trouble: for vain [is] the help of man. 108:13 Through God we
shall do valiantly: for he [it is that] shall tread down our enemies.

PSALM 109

To the chief Musician, A PSALM of David. 109:1 Hold not thy peace, O
God of my praise; 109:2 For the mouth of the wicked and the mouth of the
deceitful are opened against me: they have spoken against me with a lying
tongue. 109:3 They compassed me about also with words of hatred; and
fought against me without a cause. 109:4 For my love they are my adversaries:
but I [give myself unto] prayer. 109:5 And they have rewarded me evil for
good, and hatred for my love. 109:6 Set thou a wicked man over him: and let
Satan stand at his right hand. 109:7 When he shall be judged, let him be
condemned: and let his prayer become sin. 109:8 Let his days be few; [and]
let another take his office. 109:9 Let his children be fatherless, and his wife
a widow. 109:10 Let his children be continually vagabonds, and beg: let them
seek [their bread] also out of their desolate places. 109:11 Let the extortioner
catch all that he hath; and let the strangers spoil his labour. 109:12 Let there
be none to extend mercy unto him: neither let there be any to favour his
fatherless children. 109:13 Let his posterity be cut off; [and] in the generation
following let their name be blotted out. 109:14 Let the iniquity of his fathers
be remembered with the LORD; and let not the sin of his mother be blotted
out. 109:15 Let them be before the LORD continually, that he may cut off
the memory of them from the earth. 109:16 Because that he remembered not
to shew mercy, but persecuted the poor and needy man, that he might even

slay the broken in heart. 109:17 As he loved cursing, so let it come unto him: as he delighted not in blessing, so let it be far from him. 109:18 As he clothed himself with cursing like as with his garment, so let it come into his bowels like water, and like oil into his bones. 109:19 Let it be unto him as the garment [which] covereth him, and for a girdle wherewith he is girded continually. 109:20 [Let] this [be] the reward of mine adversaries from the LORD, and of them that speak evil against my soul. 109:21 But do thou for me, O GOD the Lord, for thy name's sake: because thy mercy [is] good, deliver thou me. 109:22 For I [am] poor and needy, and my heart is wounded within me. 109:23 I am gone like the shadow when it declineth: I am tossed up and down as the locust. 109:24 My knees are weak through fasting; and my flesh faileth of fatness. 109:25 I became also a reproach unto them: [when] they looked upon me they shaked their heads. 109:26 Help me, O LORD my God: O save me according to thy mercy: 109:27 That they may know that this [is] thy hand; [that] thou, LORD, hast done it. 109:28 Let them curse, but bless thou: when they arise, let them be ashamed; but let thy servant rejoice. 109:29 Let mine adversaries be clothed with shame, and let them cover themselves with their own confusion, as with a mantle. 109:30 I will greatly praise the LORD with my mouth; yea, I will praise him among the multitude. 109:31 For he shall stand at the right hand of the poor, to save [him] from those that condemn his soul.

PSALM 110

A PSALM of David. 110:1 The LORD said unto my Lord, Sit thou at my right hand, until I make thine enemies thy footstool. 110:2 The LORD shall send the rod of thy strength out of Zion: rule thou in the midst of thine enemies. 110:3 Thy people [shall be] willing in the day of thy power, in the beauties of holiness from the womb of the morning: thou hast the dew of thy youth. 110:4 The LORD hath sworn, and will not repent, Thou [art] a priest for ever after the order of Melchizedek. 110:5 The Lord at thy right hand shall strike through kings in the day of his wrath. 110:6 He shall judge among the heathen, he shall fill [the places] with the dead bodies; he shall wound the heads over many countries. 110:7 He shall drink of the brook in the way: therefore shall he lift up the head.

PSALM 111

111:1 Praise ye the LORD. I will praise the LORD with [my] whole heart, in the assembly of the upright, and [in] the congregation. 111:2 The works of the LORD [are] great, sought out of all them that have pleasure therein. 111:3 His work [is] honourable and glorious: and his righteousness endureth for ever. 111:4 He hath made his wonderful works to be remembered: the LORD [is] gracious and full of compassion. 111:5 He hath given meat unto them that fear him: he will ever be mindful of his covenant. 111:6 He hath shewed his people the power of his works, that he may give them the heritage of the heathen. 111:7 The works of his hands [are] verity and judgment; all his commandments [are] sure. 111:8 They stand fast for ever and ever, [and are] done in truth and uprightness. 111:9 He sent redemption unto his people: he hath commanded his covenant for ever: holy and reverend [is] his name. 111:10 The fear of the LORD [is] the beginning of wisdom: a good understanding have all they that do [his commandments]: his praise endureth for ever.

PSALM 112

112:1 Praise ye the LORD. Blessed [is] the man [that] feareth the LORD, [that] delighteth greatly in his commandments. 112:2 His seed shall be mighty upon earth: the generation of the upright shall be blessed. 112:3 Wealth and riches [shall be] in his house: and his righteousness endureth for ever. 112:4 Unto the upright there ariseth light in the darkness: [he is] gracious, and full of compassion, and righteous. 112:5 A good man sheweth favour, and lendeth: he will guide his affairs with discretion. 112:6 Surely he shall not be moved for ever: the righteous shall be in everlasting remembrance. 112:7 He shall not be afraid of evil tidings: his heart is fixed, trusting in the LORD. 112:8 His heart [is] established, he shall not be afraid, until he see [his desire] upon his enemies. 112:9 He hath dispersed, he hath

given to the poor; his righteousness endureth for ever; his horn shall be
exalted with honour. 112:10 The wicked shall see [it], and be grieved; he shall
gnash with his teeth, and melt away: the desire of the wicked shall perish.

PSALM 113
113:1 Praise ye the LORD. Praise, O ye servants of the LORD, praise the
name of the LORD. 113:2 Blessed be the name of the LORD from this time
forth and for evermore. 113:3 From the rising of the sun unto the going
down of the same the LORD's name [is] to be praised. 113:4 The LORD [is]
high above all nations, [and] his glory above the heavens. 113:5 Who [is] like
unto the LORD our God, who dwelleth on high, 113:6 Who humbleth
[himself] to behold [the things that are] in heaven, and in the earth! 113:7 He
raiseth up the poor out of the dust, [and] lifteth the needy out of the
dunghill; 113:8 That he may set [him] with princes, [even] with the princes
of his people. 113:9 He maketh the barren woman to keep house, [and to be]
a joyful mother of children. Praise ye the LORD.

PSALM 114
114:1 When Israel went out of Egypt, the house of Jacob from a people of
strange language; 114:2 Judah was his sanctuary, [and] Israel his dominion.
114:3 The sea saw [it], and fled: Jordan was driven back. 114:4 The
mountains skipped like rams, [and] the little hills like lambs. 114:5 What
[ailed] thee, O thou sea, that thou fleddest? thou Jordan, [that] thou wast
driven back? 114:6 Ye mountains, [that] ye skipped like rams; [and] ye little
hills, like lambs? 114:7 Tremble, thou earth, at the presence of the Lord, at
the presence of the God of Jacob; 114:8 Which turned the rock [into] a
standing water, the flint into a fountain of waters.

PSALM 115
115:1 Not unto us, O LORD, not unto us, but unto thy name give glory, for
thy mercy, [and] for thy truth's sake. 115:2 Wherefore should the heathen
say, Where [is] now their God? 115:3 But our God [is] in the heavens: he

hath done whatsoever he hath pleased. 115:4 Their idols [are] silver and gold,
the work of men's hands. 115:5 They have mouths, but they speak not: eyes
have they, but they see not: 115:6 They have ears, but they hear not: noses
have they, but they smell not: 115:7 They have hands, but they handle not:
feet have they, but they walk not: neither speak they through their throat.
115:8 They that make them are like unto them; [so is] every one that trusteth
in them. 115:9 O Israel, trust thou in the LORD: he [is] their help and their
shield. 115:10 O house of Aaron, trust in the LORD: he [is] their help and
their shield. 115:11 Ye that fear the LORD, trust in the LORD: he [is] their
help and their shield. 115:12 The LORD hath been mindful of us: he will
bless [us]; he will bless the house of Israel; he will bless the house of Aaron.
115:13 He will bless them that fear the LORD, [both] small and great. 115:14
The LORD shall increase you more and more, you and your children. 115:15
Ye [are] blessed of the LORD which made heaven and earth. 115:16 The
heaven, [even] the heavens, [are] the LORD's: but the earth hath he given to
the children of men. 115:17 The dead praise not the LORD, neither any that
go down into silence. 115:18 But we will bless the LORD from this time
forth and for evermore. Praise the LORD.

PSALM 116

116:1 I love the LORD, because he hath heard my voice [and] my
supplications. 116:2 Because he hath inclined his ear unto me, therefore will
I call upon [him] as long as I live. 116:3 The sorrows of death compassed me,
and the pains of hell gat hold upon me: I found trouble and sorrow. 116:4
Then called I upon the name of the LORD; O LORD, I beseech thee, deliver
my soul. 116:5 Gracious [is] the LORD, and righteous; yea, our God [is]
merciful. 116:6 The LORD preserveth the simple: I was brought low, and he
helped me. 116:7 Return unto thy rest, O my soul; for the LORD hath dealt
bountifully with thee. 116:8 For thou hast delivered my soul from death,
mine eyes from tears, [and] my feet from falling. 116:9 I will walk before the
LORD in the land of the living. 116:10 I believed, therefore have I spoken:
I was greatly afflicted: 116:11 I said in my haste, All men [are] liars. 116:12

What shall I render unto the LORD [for] all his benefits toward me? 116:13
I will take the cup of salvation, and call upon the name of the LORD. 116:14
I will pay my vows unto the LORD now in the presence of all his people.
116:15 Precious in the sight of the LORD [is] the death of his saints. 116:16
O LORD, truly I [am] thy servant; I [am] thy servant, [and] the son of thine
handmaid: thou hast loosed my bonds. 116:17 I will offer to thee the sacrifice
of thanksgiving, and will call upon the name of the LORD. 116:18 I will pay
my vows unto the LORD now in the presence of all his people, 116:19 In the
courts of the LORD's house, in the midst of thee, O Jerusalem. Praise ye the
LORD.

PSALM 117

117:1 O praise the LORD, all ye nations: praise him, all ye people. 117:2 For
his merciful kindness is great toward us: and the truth of the LORD
[endureth] for ever. Praise ye the LORD.

PSALM 118

118:1 O give thanks unto the LORD; for [he is] good: because his mercy
[endureth] for ever. 118:2 Let Israel now say, that his mercy [endureth] for
ever. 118:3 Let the house of Aaron now say, that his mercy [endureth] for
ever. 118:4 Let them now that fear the LORD say, that his mercy [endureth]
for ever. 118:5 I called upon the LORD in distress: the LORD answered me,
[and set me] in a large place. 118:6 The LORD [is] on my side; I will not fear:
what can man do unto me? 118:7 The LORD taketh my part with them that
help me: therefore shall I see [my desire] upon them that hate me. 118:8 [It
is] better to trust in the LORD than to put confidence in man. 118:9 [It is]
better to trust in the LORD than to put confidence in princes. 118:10 All
nations compassed me about: but in the name of the LORD will I destroy
them. 118:11 They compassed me about; yea, they compassed me about: but
in the name of the LORD I will destroy them. 118:12 They compassed me
about like bees; they are quenched as the fire of thorns: for in the name of
the LORD I will destroy them. 118:13 Thou hast thrust sore at me that I

might fall: but the LORD helped me. 118:14 The LORD [is] my strength and
song, and is become my salvation. 118:15 The voice of rejoicing and salvation
[is] in the tabernacles of the righteous: the right hand of the LORD doeth
valiantly. 118:16 The right hand of the LORD is exalted: the right hand of
the LORD doeth valiantly. 118:17 I shall not die, but live, and declare the
works of the LORD. 118:18 The LORD hath chastened me sore: but he hath
not given me over unto death. 118:19 Open to me the gates of righteousness:
I will go into them, [and] I will praise the LORD: 118:20 This gate of the
LORD, into which the righteous shall enter. 118:21 I will praise thee: for
thou hast heard me, and art become my salvation. 118:22 The stone [which]
the builders refused is become the head [stone] of the corner. 118:23 This is
the LORD's doing; it [is] marvellous in our eyes. 118:24 This [is] the day
[which] the LORD hath made; we will rejoice and be glad in it. 118:25 Save
now, I beseech thee, O LORD: O LORD, I beseech thee, send now
prosperity. 118:26 Blessed [be] he that cometh in the name of the LORD: we
have blessed you out of the house of the LORD. 118:27 God [is] the LORD,
which hath shewed us light: bind the sacrifice with cords, [even] unto the
horns of the altar. 118:28 Thou [art] my God, and I will praise thee: [thou
art] my God, I will exalt thee. 118:29 O give thanks unto the LORD; for [he
is] good: for his mercy [endureth] for ever.

PSALM 119

ALEPH. 119:1 Blessed [are] the undefiled in the way, who walk in the law of
the LORD. 119:2 Blessed [are] they that keep his testimonies, [and that] seek
him with the whole heart. 119:3 They also do no iniquity: they walk in his
ways. 119:4 Thou hast commanded [us] to keep thy precepts diligently. 119:5
O that my ways were directed to keep thy statutes! 119:6 Then shall I not be
ashamed, when I have respect unto all thy commandments. 119:7 I will
praise thee with uprightness of heart, when I shall have learned thy righteous
judgments. 119:8 I will keep thy statutes: O forsake me not utterly. BETH.
119:9 Wherewithal shall a young man cleanse his way? by taking heed
[thereto] according to thy word. 119:10 With my whole heart have I sought

thee: O let me not wander from thy commandments. 119:11 Thy word have I hid in mine heart, that I might not sin against thee. 119:12 Blessed [art] thou, O LORD: teach me thy statutes. 119:13 With my lihave I declared all the judgments of thy mouth. 119:14 I have rejoiced in the way of thy testimonies, as [much as] in all riches. 119:15 I will meditate in thy precepts, and have respect unto thy ways. 119:16 I will delight myself in thy statutes: I will not forget thy word. GIMEL. 119:17 Deal bountifully with thy servant, [that] I may live, and keep thy word. 119:18 Open thou mine eyes, that I may behold wondrous things out of thy law. 119:19 I [am] a stranger in the earth: hide not thy commandments from me. 119:20 My soul breaketh for the longing [that it hath] unto thy judgments at all times. 119:21 Thou hast rebuked the proud [that are] cursed, which do err from thy commandments. 119:22 Remove from me reproach and contempt; for I have kept thy testimonies. 119:23 Princes also did sit [and] speak against me: [but] thy servant did meditate in thy statutes. 119:24 Thy testimonies also [are] my delight [and] my counsellers. DALETH. 119:25 My soul cleaveth unto the dust: quicken thou me according to thy word. 119:26 I have declared my ways, and thou heardest me: teach me thy statutes. 119:27 Make me to understand the way of thy precepts: so shall I talk of thy wondrous works. 119:28 My soul melteth for heaviness: strengthen thou me according unto thy word. 119:29 Remove from me the way of lying: and grant me thy law graciously. 119:30 I have chosen the way of truth: thy judgments have I laid [before me]. 119:31 I have stuck unto thy testimonies: O LORD, put me not to shame. 119:32 I will run the way of thy commandments, when thou shalt enlarge my heart. HE. 119:33 Teach me, O LORD, the way of thy statutes; and I shall keep it [unto] the end. 119:34 Give me understanding, and I shall keep thy law; yea, I shall observe it with [my] whole heart. 119:35 Make me to go in the path of thy commandments; for therein do I delight. 119:36 Incline my heart unto thy testimonies, and not to covetousness. 119:37 Turn away mine eyes from beholding vanity; [and] quicken thou me in thy way. 119:38 Stablish thy word unto thy servant, who [is devoted] to thy fear. 119:39 Turn away my reproach which I fear: for thy judgments [are] good.

119:40 Behold, I have longed after thy precepts: quicken me in thy righteousness. VAU. 119:41 Let thy mercies come also unto me, O LORD, [even] thy salvation, according to thy word. 119:42 So shall I have wherewith to answer him that reproacheth me: for I trust in thy word. 119:43 And take not the word of truth utterly out of my mouth; for I have hoped in thy judgments. 119:44 So shall I keep thy law continually for ever and ever. 119:45 And I will walk at liberty: for I seek thy precepts. 119:46 I will speak of thy testimonies also before kings, and will not be ashamed. 119:47 And I will delight myself in thy commandments, which I have loved. 119:48 My hands also will I lift up unto thy commandments, which I have loved; and I will meditate in thy statutes. ZAIN. 119:49 Remember the word unto thy servant, upon which thou hast caused me to hope. 119:50 This [is] my comfort in my affliction: for thy word hath quickened me. 119:51 The proud have had me greatly in derision: [yet] have I not declined from thy law. 119:52 I remembered thy judgments of old, O LORD; and have comforted myself. 119:53 Horror hath taken hold upon me because of the wicked that forsake thy law. 119:54 Thy statutes have been my songs in the house of my pilgrimage. 119:55 I have remembered thy name, O LORD, in the night, and have kept thy law. 119:56 This I had, because I kept thy precepts. CHETH. 119:57 [Thou art] my portion, O LORD: I have said that I would keep thy words. 119:58 I intreated thy favour with [my] whole heart: be merciful unto me according to thy word. 119:59 I thought on my ways, and turned my feet unto thy testimonies. 119:60 I made haste, and delayed not to keep thy commandments. 119:61 The bands of the wicked have robbed me: [but] I have not forgotten thy law. 119:62 At midnight I will rise to give thanks unto thee because of thy righteous judgments. 119:63 I [am] a companion of all [them] that fear thee, and of them that keep thy precepts. 119:64 The earth, O LORD, is full of thy mercy: teach me thy statutes. TETH. 119:65 Thou hast dealt well with thy servant, O LORD, according unto thy word. 119:66 Teach me good judgment and knowledge: for I have believed thy commandments. 119:67 Before I was afflicted I went astray: but now have I kept thy word. 119:68 Thou [art] good, and doest good; teach me thy

statutes. 119:69 The proud have forged a lie against me: [but] I will keep thy
precepts with [my] whole heart. 119:70 Their heart is as fat as grease; [but] I
delight in thy law. 119:71 [It is] good for me that I have been afflicted; that
I might learn thy statutes. 119:72 The law of thy mouth [is] better unto me
than thousands of gold and silver. JOD. 119:73 Thy hands have made me
and fashioned me: give me understanding, that I may learn thy
commandments. 119:74 They that fear thee will be glad when they see me;
because I have hoped in thy word. 119:75 I know, O LORD, that thy
judgments [are] right, and [that] thou in faithfulness hast afflicted me. 119:76
Let, I pray thee, thy merciful kindness be for my comfort, according to thy
word unto thy servant. 119:77 Let thy tender mercies come unto me, that I
may live: for thy law [is] my delight. 119:78 Let the proud be ashamed; for
they dealt perversely with me without a cause: [but] I will meditate in thy
precepts. 119:79 Let those that fear thee turn unto me, and those that have
known thy testimonies. 119:80 Let my heart be sound in thy statutes; that I
be not ashamed. CAPH. 119:81 My soul fainteth for thy salvation: [but] I
hope in thy word. 119:82 Mine eyes fail for thy word, saying, When wilt thou
comfort me? 119:83 For I am become like a bottle in the smoke; [yet] do I
not forget thy statutes. 119:84 How many [are] the days of thy servant? when
wilt thou execute judgment on them that persecute me? 119:85 The proud
have digged pits for me, which [are] not after thy law. 119:86 All thy
commandments [are] faithful: they persecute me wrongfully; help thou me.
119:87 They had almost consumed me upon earth; but I forsook not thy
precepts. 119:88 Quicken me after thy lovingkindness; so shall I keep the
testimony of thy mouth. LAMED. 119:89 For ever, O LORD, thy word is
settled in heaven. 119:90 Thy faithfulness [is] unto all generations: thou hast
established the earth, and it abideth. 119:91 They continue this day
according to thine ordinances: for all [are] thy servants. 119:92 Unless thy law
[had been] my delights, I should then have perished in mine affliction.
119:93 I will never forget thy precepts: for with them thou hast quickened
me. 119:94 I [am] thine, save me; for I have sought thy precepts. 119:95 The
wicked have waited for me to destroy me: [but] I will consider thy

testimonies. 119:96 I have seen an end of all perfection: [but] thy commandment [is] exceeding broad. MEM. 119:97 O how love I thy law! it [is] my meditation all the day. 119:98 Thou through thy commandments hast made me wiser than mine enemies: for they [are] ever with me. 119:99 I have more understanding than all my teachers: for thy testimonies [are] my meditation. 119:100 I understand more than the ancients, because I keep thy precepts. 119:101 I have refrained my feet from every evil way, that I might keep thy word. 119:102 I have not departed from thy judgments: for thou hast taught me. 119:103 How sweet are thy words unto my taste! [yea, sweeter] than honey to my mouth! 119:104 Through thy precepts I get understanding: therefore I hate every false way. NUN. 119:105 Thy word [is] a lamp unto my feet, and a light unto my path. 119:106 I have sworn, and I will perform [it], that I will keep thy righteous judgments. 119:107 I am afflicted very much: quicken me, O LORD, according unto thy word. 119:108 Accept, I beseech thee, the freewill offerings of my mouth, O LORD, and teach me thy judgments. 119:109 My soul [is] continually in my hand: yet do I not forget thy law. 119:110 The wicked have laid a snare for me: yet I erred not from thy precepts. 119:111 Thy testimonies have I taken as an heritage for ever: for they [are] the rejoicing of my heart. 119:112 I have inclined mine heart to perform thy statutes alway, [even unto] the end. SAMECH. 119:113 I hate [vain] thoughts: but thy law do I love. 119:114 Thou [art] my hiding place and my shield: I hope in thy word. 119:115 Depart from me, ye evildoers: for I will keep the commandments of my God. 119:116 Uphold me according unto thy word, that I may live: and let me not be ashamed of my hope. 119:117 Hold thou me up, and I shall be safe: and I will have respect unto thy statutes continually. 119:118 Thou hast trodden down all them that err from thy statutes: for their deceit [is] falsehood. 119:119 Thou puttest away all the wicked of the earth [like] dross: therefore I love thy testimonies. 119:120 My flesh trembleth for fear of thee; and I am afraid of thy judgments. AIN. 119:121 I have done judgment and justice: leave me not to mine oppressors. 119:122 Be surety for thy servant for good: let not the proud oppress me. 119:123 Mine eyes fail for thy salvation, and for the word of thy righteousness. 119:124 Deal with thy servant according unto thy mercy, and teach me thy statutes. 119:125 I [am] thy servant; give me understanding, that I may know thy testimonies. 119:126 [It is] time for [thee], LORD, to work: [for] they have made void thy law. 119:127 Therefore I love thy commandments above gold; yea, above fine gold. 119:128 Therefore I esteem all [thy] precepts [concerning] all [things to be] right; [and] I hate every false way. PE. 119:129 Thy testimonies [are] wonderful: therefore doth my soul keep them. 119:130 The entrance of thy words giveth light; it giveth understanding unto the simple. 119:131 I opened my mouth, and panted: for I longed for thy commandments. 119:132 Look thou upon me, and be merciful unto me, as thou usest to do unto those that love thy name. 119:133 Order my stein thy word: and let not any iniquity have dominion over me. 119:134 Deliver me from the oppression of man: so will I keep thy precepts. 119:135 Make thy face to shine upon thy servant; and teach me thy statutes. 119:136 Rivers of waters run down mine eyes, because they keep not thy law. TZADDI. 119:137 Righteous [art] thou, O LORD, and upright [are] thy judgments. 119:138 Thy testimonies [that] thou hast commanded [are] righteous and very faithful. 119:139 My zeal hath consumed me, because mine enemies have forgotten thy words. 119:140 Thy word [is] very pure: therefore thy servant loveth it. 119:141 I [am] small and despised: [yet] do not I forget thy precepts. 119:142 Thy righteousness [is] an everlasting righteousness, and thy law [is] the truth. 119:143 Trouble and anguish have taken hold on me: [yet] thy commandments [are] my delights. 119:144 The righteousness of thy testimonies [is] everlasting: give me understanding, and I shall live. KOPH. 119:145 I cried with [my] whole heart; hear me, O LORD: I will keep thy statutes. 119:146 I cried unto thee; save me, and I shall keep thy testimonies. 119:147 I prevented the dawning of the morning, and cried: I hoped in thy word. 119:148 Mine eyes prevent the [night] watches, that I might meditate in thy word. 119:149 Hear my voice according unto thy lovingkindness: O LORD, quicken me according to thy judgment. 119:150 They draw nigh that follow after mischief: they are far from thy law. 119:151 Thou [art] near, O LORD; and all thy commandments [are] truth.

119:152 Concerning thy testimonies, I have known of old that thou hast founded them for ever. RESH. 119:153 Consider mine affliction, and deliver me: for I do not forget thy law. 119:154 Plead my cause, and deliver me: quicken me according to thy word. 119:155 Salvation [is] far from the wicked: for they seek not thy statutes. 119:156 Great [are] thy tender mercies, O LORD: quicken me according to thy judgments. 119:157 Many [are] my persecutors and mine enemies; [yet] do I not decline from thy testimonies. 119:158 I beheld the transgressors, and was grieved; because they kept not thy word. 119:159 Consider how I love thy precepts: quicken me, O LORD, according to thy lovingkindness. 119:160 Thy word [is] true [from] the beginning: and every one of thy righteous judgments [endureth] for ever. SCHIN. 119:161 Princes have persecuted me without a cause: but my heart standeth in awe of thy word. 119:162 I rejoice at thy word, as one that findeth great spoil. 119:163 I hate and abhor lying: [but] thy law do I love. 119:164 Seven times a day do I praise thee because of thy righteous judgments. 119:165 Great peace have they which love thy law: and nothing shall offend them. 119:166 LORD, I have hoped for thy salvation, and done thy commandments. 119:167 My soul hath kept thy testimonies; and I love them exceedingly. 119:168 I have kept thy precepts and thy testimonies: for all my ways [are] before thee. TAU. 119:169 Let my cry come near before thee, O LORD: give me understanding according to thy word. 119:170 Let my supplication come before thee: deliver me according to thy word. 119:171 My lishall utter praise, when thou hast taught me thy statutes. 119:172 My tongue shall speak of thy word: for all thy commandments [are] righteousness. 119:173 Let thine hand help me; for I have chosen thy precepts. 119:174 I have longed for thy salvation, O LORD; and thy law [is] my delight. 119:175 Let my soul live, and it shall praise thee; and let thy judgments help me. 119:176 I have gone astray like a lost sheep; seek thy servant; for I do not forget thy commandments.

PSALM 120

A Song of degrees. 120:1 In my distress I cried unto the LORD, and he heard me. 120:2 Deliver my soul, O LORD, from lying lips, [and] from a deceitful tongue. 120:3 What shall be given unto thee? or what shall be done unto thee, thou false tongue? 120:4 Sharp arrows of the mighty, with coals of juniper. 120:5 Woe is me, that I sojourn in Mesech, [that] I dwell in the tents of Kedar! 120:6 My soul hath long dwelt with him that hateth peace. 120:7 I [am for] peace: but when I speak, they [are] for war.

PSALM 121

A Song of degrees. 121:1 I will lift up mine eyes unto the hills, from whence cometh my help. 121:2 My help [cometh] from the LORD, which made heaven and earth. 121:3 He will not suffer thy foot to be moved: he that keepeth thee will not slumber. 121:4 Behold, he that keepeth Israel shall neither slumber nor sleep. 121:5 The LORD [is] thy keeper: the LORD [is] thy shade upon thy right hand. 121:6 The sun shall not smite thee by day, nor the moon by night. 121:7 The LORD shall preserve thee from all evil: he shall preserve thy soul. 121:8 The LORD shall preserve thy going out and thy coming in from this time forth, and even for evermore.

PSALM 122

A Song of degrees of David. 122:1 I was glad when they said unto me, Let us go into the house of the LORD. 122:2 Our feet shall stand within thy gates, O Jerusalem. 122:3 Jerusalem is builded as a city that is compact together: 122:4 Whither the tribes go up, the tribes of the LORD, unto the testimony of Israel, to give thanks unto the name of the LORD. 122:5 For there are set thrones of judgment, the thrones of the house of David. 122:6 Pray for the peace of Jerusalem: they shall prosper that love thee. 122:7 Peace be within thy walls, [and] prosperity within thy palaces. 122:8 For my brethren and companions' sakes, I will now say, Peace [be] within thee. 122:9 Because of the house of the LORD our God I will seek thy good.

PSALM 123

A Song of degrees. 123:1 Unto thee lift I up mine eyes, O thou that dwellest

in the heavens. 123:2 Behold, as the eyes of servants [look] unto the hand of
their masters, [and] as the eyes of a maiden unto the hand of her mistress; so
our eyes [wait] upon the LORD our God, until that he have mercy upon us.
123:3 Have mercy upon us, O LORD, have mercy upon us: for we are
exceedingly filled with contempt. 123:4 Our soul is exceedingly filled with
the scorning of those that are at ease, [and] with the contempt of the proud.

PSALM 124

A Song of degrees of David. 124:1 If [it had] not [been] the LORD who was
on our side, now may Israel say; 124:2 If [it had] not [been] the LORD who
was on our side, when men rose up against us: 124:3 Then they had
swallowed us up quick, when their wrath was kindled against us: 124:4 Then
the waters had overwhelmed us, the stream had gone over our soul: 124:5
Then the proud waters had gone over our soul. 124:6 Blessed [be] the
LORD, who hath not given us [as] a prey to their teeth. 124:7 Our soul is
escaped as a bird out of the snare of the fowlers: the snare is broken, and we
are escaped. 124:8 Our help [is] in the name of the LORD, who made heaven
and earth.

PSALM 125

A Song of degrees. 125:1 They that trust in the LORD [shall be] as mount
Zion, [which] cannot be removed, [but] abideth for ever. 125:2 [As] the
mountains [are] round about Jerusalem, so the LORD [is] round about his
people from henceforth even for ever. 125:3 For the rod of the wicked shall
not rest upon the lot of the righteous; lest the righteous put forth their hands
unto iniquity. 125:4 Do good, O LORD, unto [those that be] good, and to
[them that are] upright in their hearts. 125:5 As for such as turn aside unto
their crooked ways, the LORD shall lead them forth with the workers of
iniquity: [but] peace [shall be] upon Israel.

PSALM 126

A Song of degrees. 126:1 When the LORD turned again the captivity of

Zion, we were like them that dream. 126:2 Then was our mouth filled with laughter, and our tongue with singing: then said they among the heathen, The LORD hath done great things for them. 126:3 The LORD hath done great things for us; [whereof] we are glad. 126:4 Turn again our captivity, O LORD, as the streams in the south. 126:5 They that sow in tears shall reap in joy. 126:6 He that goeth forth and weepeth, bearing precious seed, shall doubtless come again with rejoicing, bringing his sheaves [with him].

PSALM 127

A Song of degrees for Solomon. 127:1 Except the LORD build the house, they labour in vain that build it: except the LORD keep the city, the watchman waketh [but] in vain. 127:2 [It is] vain for you to rise up early, to sit up late, to eat the bread of sorrows: [for] so he giveth his beloved sleep. 127:3 Lo, children [are] an heritage of the LORD: [and] the fruit of the womb [is his] reward. 127:4 As arrows [are] in the hand of a mighty man; so [are] children of the youth. 127:5 Happy [is] the man that hath his quiver full of them: they shall not be ashamed, but they shall speak with the enemies in the gate.

PSALM 128

A Song of degrees. 128:1 Blessed [is] every one that feareth the LORD; that walketh in his ways. 128:2 For thou shalt eat the labour of thine hands: happy [shalt] thou [be], and [it shall be] well with thee. 128:3 Thy wife [shall be] as a fruitful vine by the sides of thine house: thy children like olive plants round about thy table. 128:4 Behold, that thus shall the man be blessed that feareth the LORD. 128:5 The LORD shall bless thee out of Zion: and thou shalt see the good of Jerusalem all the days of thy life. 128:6 Yea, thou shalt see thy children's children, [and] peace upon Israel.

PSALM 129

A Song of degrees. 129:1 Many a time have they afflicted me from my youth, may Israel now say: 129:2 Many a time have they afflicted me from my youth:

yet they have not prevailed against me. 129:3 The plowers plowed upon my back: they made long their furrows. 129:4 The LORD [is] righteous: he hath cut asunder the cords of the wicked. 129:5 Let them all be confounded and turned back that hate Zion. 129:6 Let them be as the grass [upon] the housetops, which withereth afore it groweth up: 129:7 Wherewith the mower filleth not his hand; nor he that bindeth sheaves his bosom. 129:8 Neither do they which go by say, The blessing of the LORD [be] upon you: we bless you in the name of the LORD.

PSALM 130
A Song of degrees. 130:1 Out of the depths have I cried unto thee, O LORD. 130:2 Lord, hear my voice: let thine ears be attentive to the voice of my supplications. 130:3 If thou, LORD, shouldest mark iniquities, O Lord, who shall stand? 130:4 But [there is] forgiveness with thee, that thou mayest be feared. 130:5 I wait for the LORD, my soul doth wait, and in his word do I hope. 130:6 My soul [waiteth] for the Lord more than they that watch for the morning: [I say, more than] they that watch for the morning. 130:7 Let Israel hope in the LORD: for with the LORD [there is] mercy, and with him [is] plenteous redemption. 130:8 And he shall redeem Israel from all his iniquities.

PSALM 131
A Song of degrees of David. 131:1 LORD, my heart is not haughty, nor mine eyes lofty: neither do I exercise myself in great matters, or in things too high for me. 131:2 Surely I have behaved and quieted myself, as a child that is weaned of his mother: my soul [is] even as a weaned child. 131:3 Let Israel hope in the LORD from henceforth and for ever.

PSALM 132
A Song of degrees. 132:1 LORD, remember David, [and] all his afflictions: 132:2 How he sware unto the LORD, [and] vowed unto the mighty [God] of Jacob; 132:3 Surely I will not come into the tabernacle of my house, nor go

up into my bed; 132:4 I will not give sleep to mine eyes, [or] slumber to mine eyelids, 132:5 Until I find out a place for the LORD, an habitation for the mighty [God] of Jacob. 132:6 Lo, we heard of it at Ephratah: we found it in the fields of the wood. 132:7 We will go into his tabernacles: we will worship at his footstool. 132:8 Arise, O LORD, into thy rest; thou, and the ark of thy strength. 132:9 Let thy priests be clothed with righteousness; and let thy saints shout for joy. 132:10 For thy servant David's sake turn not away the face of thine anointed. 132:11 The LORD hath sworn [in] truth unto David; he will not turn from it; Of the fruit of thy body will I set upon thy throne. 132:12 If thy children will keep my covenant and my testimony that I shall teach them, their children shall also sit upon thy throne for evermore. 132:13 For the LORD hath chosen Zion; he hath desired [it] for his habitation. 132:14 This [is] my rest for ever: here will I dwell; for I have desired it. 132:15 I will abundantly bless her provision: I will satisfy her poor with bread. 132:16 I will also clothe her priests with salvation: and her saints shall shout aloud for joy. 132:17 There will I make the horn of David to bud: I have ordained a lamp for mine anointed. 132:18 His enemies will I clothe with shame: but upon himself shall his crown flourish.

PSALM 133

A Song of degrees of David. 133:1 Behold, how good and how pleasant [it is] for brethren to dwell together in unity! 133:2 [It is] like the precious ointment upon the head, that ran down upon the beard, [even] Aaron's beard: that went down to the skirts of his garments; 133:3 As the dew of Hermon, [and as the dew] that descended upon the mountains of Zion: for there the LORD commanded the blessing, [even] life for evermore.

PSALM 134

A Song of degrees. 134:1 Behold, bless ye the LORD, all [ye] servants of the LORD, which by night stand in the house of the LORD. 134:2 Lift up your hands [in] the sanctuary, and bless the LORD. 134:3 The LORD that made heaven and earth bless thee out of Zion.

PSALM 135
135:1 Praise ye the LORD. Praise ye the name of the LORD; praise [him], O
ye servants of the LORD. 135:2 Ye that stand in the house of the LORD, in
the courts of the house of our God, 135:3 Praise the LORD; for the LORD
[is] good: sing praises unto his name; for [it is] pleasant. 135:4 For the LORD
hath chosen Jacob unto himself, [and] Israel for his peculiar treasure. 135:5
For I know that the LORD [is] great, and [that] our Lord [is] above all gods.
135:6 Whatsoever the LORD pleased, [that] did he in heaven, and in earth,
in the seas, and all deep places. 135:7 He causeth the vapours to ascend from
the ends of the earth; he maketh lightnings for the rain; he bringeth the wind
out of his treasuries. 135:8 Who smote the firstborn of Egypt, both of man
and beast. 135:9 [Who] sent tokens and wonders into the midst of thee, O
Egypt, upon Pharaoh, and upon all his servants. 135:10 Who smote great
nations, and slew mighty kings; 135:11 Sihon king of the Amorites, and Og
king of Bashan, and all the kingdoms of Canaan: 135:12 And gave their land
[for] an heritage, an heritage unto Israel his people. 135:13 Thy name, O
LORD, [endureth] for ever; [and] thy memorial, O LORD, throughout all
generations. 135:14 For the LORD will judge his people, and he will repent
himself concerning his servants. 135:15 The idols of the heathen [are] silver
and gold, the work of men's hands. 135:16 They have mouths, but they speak
not; eyes have they, but they see not; 135:17 They have ears, but they hear
not; neither is there [any] breath in their mouths. 135:18 They that make
them are like unto them: [so is] every one that trusteth in them. 135:19 Bless
the LORD, O house of Israel: bless the LORD, O house of Aaron: 135:20
Bless the LORD, O house of Levi: ye that fear the LORD, bless the LORD.
135:21 Blessed be the LORD out of Zion, which dwelleth at Jerusalem. Praise
ye the LORD.

PSALM 136
136:1 O give thanks unto the LORD; for [he is] good: for his mercy
[endureth] for ever. 136:2 O give thanks unto the God of gods: for his mercy
[endureth] for ever. 136:3 O give thanks to the Lord of lords: for his mercy

[endureth] for ever. 136:4 To him who alone doeth great wonders: for his mercy [endureth] for ever. 136:5 To him that by wisdom made the heavens: for his mercy [endureth] for ever. 136:6 To him that stretched out the earth above the waters: for his mercy [endureth] for ever. 136:7 To him that made great lights: for his mercy [endureth] for ever: 136:8 The sun to rule by day: for his mercy [endureth] for ever: 136:9 The moon and stars to rule by night: for his mercy [endureth] for ever. 136:10 To him that smote Egypt in their firstborn: for his mercy [endureth] for ever: 136:11 And brought out Israel from among them: for his mercy [endureth] for ever: 136:12 With a strong hand, and with a stretched out arm: for his mercy [endureth] for ever. 136:13 To him which divided the Red sea into parts: for his mercy [endureth] for ever: 136:14 And made Israel to pass through the midst of it: for his mercy [endureth] for ever: 136:15 But overthrew Pharaoh and his host in the Red sea: for his mercy [endureth] for ever. 136:16 To him which led his people through the wilderness: for his mercy [endureth] for ever. 136:17 To him which smote great kings: for his mercy [endureth] for ever: 136:18 And slew famous kings: for his mercy [endureth] for ever: 136:19 Sihon king of the Amorites: for his mercy [endureth] for ever: 136:20 And Og the king of Bashan: for his mercy [endureth] for ever: 136:21 And gave their land for an heritage: for his mercy [endureth] for ever: 136:22 [Even] an heritage unto Israel his servant: for his mercy [endureth] for ever. 136:23 Who remembered us in our low estate: for his mercy [endureth] for ever: 136:24 And hath redeemed us from our enemies: for his mercy [endureth] for ever. 136:25 Who giveth food to all flesh: for his mercy [endureth] for ever. 136:26 O give thanks unto the God of heaven: for his mercy [endureth] for ever.

PSALM 137

137:1 By the rivers of Babylon, there we sat down, yea, we wept, when we remembered Zion. 137:2 We hanged our harupon the willows in the midst thereof. 137:3 For there they that carried us away captive required of us a song; and they that wasted us [required of us] mirth, [saying], Sing us [one] of the songs of Zion. 137:4 How shall we sing the LORD's song in a strange land? 137:5 If I forget thee, O Jerusalem, let my right hand forget [her cunning]. 137:6 If I do not remember thee, let my tongue cleave to the roof of my mouth; if I prefer not Jerusalem above my chief joy. 137:7 Remember, O LORD, the children of Edom in the day of Jerusalem; who said, Rase [it], rase [it, even] to the foundation thereof. 137:8 O daughter of Babylon, who art to be destroyed; happy [shall he be], that rewardeth thee as thou hast served us. 137:9 Happy [shall he be], that taketh and dasheth thy little ones against the stones.

PSALM 138

[A PSALM] of David. 138:1 I will praise thee with my whole heart: before the gods will I sing praise unto thee. 138:2 I will worship toward thy holy temple, and praise thy name for thy lovingkindness and for thy truth: for thou hast magnified thy word above all thy name. 138:3 In the day when I cried thou answeredst me, [and] strengthenedst me [with] strength in my soul. 138:4 All the kings of the earth shall praise thee, O LORD, when they hear the words of thy mouth. 138:5 Yea, they shall sing in the ways of the LORD: for great [is] the glory of the LORD. 138:6 Though the LORD [be] high, yet hath he respect unto the lowly: but the proud he knoweth afar off. 138:7 Though I walk in the midst of trouble, thou wilt revive me: thou shalt stretch forth thine hand against the wrath of mine enemies, and thy right hand shall save me. 138:8 The LORD will perfect [that which] concerneth me: thy mercy, O LORD, [endureth] for ever: forsake not the works of thine own hands.

PSALM 139

To the chief Musician, A PSALM of David. 139:1 O LORD, thou hast searched me, and known [me]. 139:2 Thou knowest my downsitting and mine uprising, thou understandest my thought afar off. 139:3 Thou compassest my path and my lying down, and art acquainted [with] all my ways. 139:4 For [there is] not a word in my tongue, [but], lo, O LORD, thou knowest it altogether. 139:5 Thou hast beset me behind and before, and laid thine hand upon me. 139:6 [Such] knowledge [is] too wonderful for me; it is high, I cannot [attain] unto it. 139:7 Whither shall I go from thy spirit? or whither shall I flee from thy presence? 139:8 If I ascend up into heaven, thou [art] there: if I make my bed in hell, behold, thou [art there]. 139:9 [If] I take the wings of the morning, [and] dwell in the uttermost parts of the sea; 139:10 Even there shall thy hand lead me, and thy right hand shall hold me. 139:11 If I say, Surely the darkness shall cover me; even the night shall be light about me. 139:12 Yea, the darkness hideth not from thee; but the night shineth as the day: the darkness and the light [are] both alike [to thee]. 139:13 For thou hast possessed my reins: thou hast covered me in my mother's womb. 139:14 I will praise thee; for I am fearfully [and] wonderfully made: marvellous [are] thy works; and [that] my soul knoweth right well. 139:15 My substance was not hid from thee, when I was made in secret, [and] curiously wrought in the lowest parts of the earth. 139:16 Thine eyes did see my substance, yet being unperfect; and in thy book all [my members] were written, [which] in continuance were fashioned, when [as yet there was] none of them. 139:17 How precious also are thy thoughts unto me, O God! how great is the sum of them! 139:18 [If] I should count them, they are more in number than the sand: when I awake, I am still with thee. 139:19 Surely thou wilt slay the wicked, O God: depart from me therefore, ye bloody men. 139:20 For they speak against thee wickedly, [and] thine enemies take [thy name] in vain. 139:21 Do not I hate them, O LORD, that hate thee? and am not I grieved with those that rise up against thee? 139:22 I hate them with perfect hatred: I count them mine enemies. 139:23 Search me, O God, and know my heart: try me, and know my thoughts: 139:24 And see if [there be any] wicked way in me, and lead me in the way everlasting.

PSALM 140

To the chief Musician, A PSALM of David. 140:1 Deliver me, O LORD, from the evil man: preserve me from the violent man; 140:2 Which imagine mischiefs in [their] heart; continually are they gathered together [for] war. 140:3 They have sharpened their tongues like a serpent; adders' poison [is] under their lips. Selah. 140:4 Keep me, O LORD, from the hands of the

wicked; preserve me from the violent man; who have purposed to overthrow
my goings. 140:5 The proud have hid a snare for me, and cords; they have
spread a net by the wayside; they have set gins for me. Selah. 140:6 I said
unto the LORD, Thou [art] my God: hear the voice of my supplications, O
LORD. 140:7 O GOD the Lord, the strength of my salvation, thou hast
covered my head in the day of battle. 140:8 Grant not, O LORD, the desires
of the wicked: further not his wicked device; [lest] they exalt themselves.
Selah. 140:9 [As for] the head of those that compass me about, let the
mischief of their own licover them. 140:10 Let burning coals fall upon them:
let them be cast into the fire; into deep pits, that they rise not up again.
140:11 Let not an evil speaker be established in the earth: evil shall hunt the
violent man to overthrow [him]. 140:12 I know that the LORD will maintain
the cause of the afflicted, [and] the right of the poor. 140:13 Surely the
righteous shall give thanks unto thy name: the upright shall dwell in thy
presence.

PSALM 141

A PSALM of David. 141:1 LORD, I cry unto thee: make haste unto me; give
ear unto my voice, when I cry unto thee. 141:2 Let my prayer be set forth
before thee [as] incense; [and] the lifting up of my hands [as] the evening
sacrifice. 141:3 Set a watch, O LORD, before my mouth; keep the door of my
lips. 141:4 Incline not my heart to [any] evil thing, to practise wicked works
with men that work iniquity: and let me not eat of their dainties. 141:5 Let
the righteous smite me; [it shall be] a kindness: and let him reprove me; [it
shall be] an excellent oil, [which] shall not break my head: for yet my prayer
also [shall be] in their calamities. 141:6 When their judges are overthrown in
stony places, they shall hear my words; for they are sweet. 141:7 Our bones
are scattered at the grave's mouth, as when one cutteth and cleaveth [wood]
upon the earth. 141:8 But mine eyes [are] unto thee, O GOD the Lord: in
thee is my trust; leave not my soul destitute. 141:9 Keep me from the snares
[which] they have laid for me, and the gins of the workers of iniquity. 141:10
Let the wicked fall into their own nets, whilst that I withal escape.

PSALM 142

Maschil of David; A Prayer when he was in the cave. 142:1 I cried unto the LORD with my voice; with my voice unto the LORD did I make my supplication. 142:2 I poured out my complaint before him; I shewed before him my trouble. 142:3 When my spirit was overwhelmed within me, then thou knewest my path. In the way wherein I walked have they privily laid a snare for me. 142:4 I looked on [my] right hand, and beheld, but [there was] no man that would know me: refuge failed me; no man cared for my soul. 142:5 I cried unto thee, O LORD: I said, Thou [art] my refuge [and] my portion in the land of the living. 142:6 Attend unto my cry; for I am brought very low: deliver me from my persecutors; for they are stronger than I. 142:7 Bring my soul out of prison, that I may praise thy name: the righteous shall compass me about; for thou shalt deal bountifully with me.

PSALM 143

A PSALM of David. 143:1 Hear my prayer, O LORD, give ear to my supplications: in thy faithfulness answer me, [and] in thy righteousness. 143:2 And enter not into judgment with thy servant: for in thy sight shall no man living be justified. 143:3 For the enemy hath persecuted my soul; he hath smitten my life down to the ground; he hath made me to dwell in darkness, as those that have been long dead. 143:4 Therefore is my spirit overwhelmed within me; my heart within me is desolate. 143:5 I remember the days of old; I meditate on all thy works; I muse on the work of thy hands. 143:6 I stretch forth my hands unto thee: my soul [thirsteth] after thee, as a thirsty land. Selah. 143:7 Hear me speedily, O LORD: my spirit faileth: hide not thy face from me, lest I be like unto them that go down into the pit. 143:8 Cause me to hear thy lovingkindness in the morning; for in thee do I trust: cause me to know the way wherein I should walk; for I lift up my soul unto thee. 143:9 Deliver me, O LORD, from mine enemies: I flee unto thee to hide me. 143:10 Teach me to do thy will; for thou [art] my God: thy spirit [is] good; lead me into the land of uprightness. 143:11 Quicken me, O LORD, for thy name's sake: for thy righteousness' sake bring my soul out of trouble. 143:12

And of thy mercy cut off mine enemies, and destroy all them that afflict my soul: for I [am] thy servant.

PSALM 144

[A PSALM] of David. 144:1 Blessed [be] the LORD my strength, which teacheth my hands to war, [and] my fingers to fight: 144:2 My goodness, and my fortress; my high tower, and my deliverer; my shield, and [he] in whom I trust; who subdueth my people under me. 144:3 LORD, what [is] man, that thou takest knowledge of him! [or] the son of man, that thou makest account of him! 144:4 Man is like to vanity: his days [are] as a shadow that passeth away. 144:5 Bow thy heavens, O LORD, and come down: touch the mountains, and they shall smoke. 144:6 Cast forth lightning, and scatter them: shoot out thine arrows, and destroy them. 144:7 Send thine hand from above; rid me, and deliver me out of great waters, from the hand of strange children; 144:8 Whose mouth speaketh vanity, and their right hand [is] a right hand of falsehood. 144:9 I will sing a new song unto thee, O God: upon a psaltery [and] an instrument of ten strings will I sing praises unto thee. 144:10 [It is he] that giveth salvation unto kings: who delivereth David his servant from the hurtful sword. 144:11 Rid me, and deliver me from the hand of strange children, whose mouth speaketh vanity, and their right hand [is] a right hand of falsehood: 144:12 That our sons [may be] as plants grown up in their youth; [that] our daughters [may be] as corner stones, polished [after] the similitude of a palace: 144:13 [That] our garners [may be] full, affording all manner of store: [that] our sheep may bring forth thousands and ten thousands in our streets: 144:14 [That] our oxen [may be] strong to labour; [that there be] no breaking in, nor going out; that [there be] no complaining in our streets. 144:15 Happy [is that] people, that is in such a case: [yea], happy [is that] people, whose God [is] the LORD.

PSALM 145

David's [PSALM] of praise. 145:1 I will extol thee, my God, O king; and I will bless thy name for ever and ever. 145:2 Every day will I bless thee; and I will

praise thy name for ever and ever. 145:3 Great [is] the LORD, and greatly to
be praised; and his greatness [is] unsearchable. 145:4 One generation shall
praise thy works to another, and shall declare thy mighty acts. 145:5 I will
speak of the glorious honour of thy majesty, and of thy wondrous works.
145:6 And [men] shall speak of the might of thy terrible acts: and I will
declare thy greatness. 145:7 They shall abundantly utter the memory of thy
great goodness, and shall sing of thy righteousness. 145:8 The LORD [is]
gracious, and full of compassion; slow to anger, and of great mercy. 145:9
The LORD [is] good to all: and his tender mercies [are] over all his works.
145:10 All thy works shall praise thee, O LORD; and thy saints shall bless
thee. 145:11 They shall speak of the glory of thy kingdom, and talk of thy
power; 145:12 To make known to the sons of men his mighty acts, and the
glorious majesty of his kingdom. 145:13 Thy kingdom [is] an everlasting
kingdom, and thy dominion [endureth] throughout all generations. 145:14
The LORD upholdeth all that fall, and raiseth up all [those that be] bowed
down. 145:15 The eyes of all wait upon thee; and thou givest them their meat
in due season. 145:16 Thou openest thine hand, and satisfiest the desire of
every living thing. 145:17 The LORD [is] righteous in all his ways, and holy
in all his works. 145:18 The LORD [is] nigh unto all them that call upon
him, to all that call upon him in truth. 145:19 He will fulfil the desire of
them that fear him: he also will hear their cry, and will save them. 145:20
The LORD preserveth all them that love him: but all the wicked will he
destroy. 145:21 My mouth shall speak the praise of the LORD: and let all
flesh bless his holy name for ever and ever.

PSALM 146

146:1 Praise ye the LORD. Praise the LORD, O my soul. 146:2 While I live
will I praise the LORD: I will sing praises unto my God while I have any
being. 146:3 Put not your trust in princes, [nor] in the son of man, in whom
[there is] no help. 146:4 His breath goeth forth, he returneth to his earth; in
that very day his thoughts perish. 146:5 Happy [is he] that [hath] the God of
Jacob for his help, whose hope [is] in the LORD his God: 146:6 Which made

heaven, and earth, the sea, and all that therein [is]: which keepeth truth for ever: 146:7 Which executeth judgment for the oppressed: which giveth food to the hungry. The LORD looseth the prisoners: 146:8 The LORD openeth [the eyes of] the blind: the LORD raiseth them that are bowed down: the LORD loveth the righteous: 146:9 The LORD preserveth the strangers; he relieveth the fatherless and widow: but the way of the wicked he turneth upside down. 146:10 The LORD shall reign for ever, [even] thy God, O Zion, unto all generations. Praise ye the LORD.

PSALM 147

147:1 Praise ye the LORD: for [it is] good to sing praises unto our God; for [it is] pleasant; [and] praise is comely. 147:2 The LORD doth build up Jerusalem: he gathereth together the outcasts of Israel. 147:3 He healeth the broken in heart, and bindeth up their wounds. 147:4 He telleth the number of the stars; he calleth them all by [their] names. 147:5 Great [is] our Lord, and of great power: his understanding [is] infinite. 147:6 The LORD lifteth up the meek: he casteth the wicked down to the ground. 147:7 Sing unto the LORD with thanksgiving; sing praise upon the harp unto our God: 147:8 Who covereth the heaven with clouds, who prepareth rain for the earth, who maketh grass to grow upon the mountains. 147:9 He giveth to the beast his food, [and] to the young ravens which cry. 147:10 He delighteth not in the strength of the horse: he taketh not pleasure in the legs of a man. 147:11 The LORD taketh pleasure in them that fear him, in those that hope in his mercy. 147:12 Praise the LORD, O Jerusalem; praise thy God, O Zion. 147:13 For he hath strengthened the bars of thy gates; he hath blessed thy children within thee. 147:14 He maketh peace [in] thy borders, [and] filleth thee with the finest of the wheat. 147:15 He sendeth forth his commandment [upon] earth: his word runneth very swiftly. 147:16 He giveth snow like wool: he scattereth the hoarfrost like ashes. 147:17 He casteth forth his ice like morsels: who can stand before his cold? 147:18 He sendeth out his word, and melteth them: he causeth his wind to blow, [and] the waters flow. 147:19 He sheweth his word unto Jacob, his statutes and his judgments

unto Israel. 147:20 He hath not dealt so with any nation: and [as for his]
judgments, they have not known them. Praise ye the LORD.

PSALM 148
148:1 Praise ye the LORD. Praise ye the LORD from the heavens: praise him
in the heights. 148:2 Praise ye him, all his angels: praise ye him, all his hosts.
148:3 Praise ye him, sun and moon: praise him, all ye stars of light. 148:4
Praise him, ye heavens of heavens, and ye waters that [be] above the heavens.
148:5 Let them praise the name of the LORD: for he commanded, and they
were created. 148:6 He hath also stablished them for ever and ever: he hath
made a decree which shall not pass. 148:7 Praise the LORD from the earth,
ye dragons, and all deeps: 148:8 Fire, and hail; snow, and vapour; stormy
wind fulfilling his word: 148:9 Mountains, and all hills; fruitful trees, and all
cedars: 148:10 Beasts, and all cattle; creeping things, and flying fowl: 148:11
Kings of the earth, and all people; princes, and all judges of the earth: 148:12
Both young men, and maidens; old men, and children: 148:13 Let them
praise the name of the LORD: for his name alone is excellent; his glory [is]
above the earth and heaven. 148:14 He also exalteth the horn of his people,
the praise of all his saints; [even] of the children of Israel, a people near unto
him. Praise ye the LORD.

PSALM 149
149:1 Praise ye the LORD. Sing unto the LORD a new song, [and] his praise
in the congregation of saints. 149:2 Let Israel rejoice in him that made him:
let the children of Zion be joyful in their King. 149:3 Let them praise his
name in the dance: let them sing praises unto him with the timbrel and harp.
149:4 For the LORD taketh pleasure in his people: he will beautify the meek
with salvation. 149:5 Let the saints be joyful in glory: let them sing aloud
upon their beds. 149:6 [Let] the high [praises] of God [be] in their mouth,
and a twoedged sword in their hand; 149:7 To execute vengeance upon the
heathen, [and] punishments upon the people; 149:8 To bind their kings with
chains, and their nobles with fetters of iron; 149:9 To execute upon them the

judgment written: this honour have all his saints. Praise ye the LORD.

PSALM 150
150:1 Praise ye the LORD. Praise God in his sanctuary: praise him in the
firmament of his power. 150:2 Praise him for his mighty acts: praise him
according to his excellent greatness. 150:3 Praise him with the sound of the
trumpet: praise him with the psaltery and harp. 150:4 Praise him with the
timbrel and dance: praise him with stringed instruments and organs. 150:5
Praise him upon the loud cymbals: praise him upon the high sounding
cymbals. 150:6 Let every thing that hath breath praise the LORD. Praise ye
the LORD.

Other books in this series available from Sublime Books.

The Old Testament

978-1-5154-4078-9 The First Book of Moses: Genesis
978-1-5154-4079-6 The Second Book of Moses: Exodus
978-1-5154-4080-2 L The Third Book of Moses: Leviticus
978-1-5154-4081-9 The Fourth Book of Moses: Numbers
978-1-5154-4082-6 The Fifth Book of Moses: Deuteronomy
978-1-5154-4083-3 The Book of Joshua
978-1-5154-4084-0 The Book of Judges
978-1-5154-4085-7 The Book of Ruth
978-1-5154-4086-4 The First Book of Samuel
978-1-5154-4087-1 The Second Book of Samuel
978-1-5154-4088-8 The First Book of the Kings
978-1-5154-4089-5 The Second Book of the Kings
978-1-5154-4090-1 The First Book of the Chronicles
978-1-5154-4091-8 The Second Book of the Chronicles
978-1-5154-4092-5 The Book of Ezra
978-1-5154-4093-2 The Book of Nehemiah
978-1-5154-4094-9 The Book of Esther
978-1-5154-4095-6 The Book of Job
978-1-5154-4096-3 The Book of Psalms
978-1-5154-4097-0 The Proverbs
978-1-5154-4098-7 The Book of Ecclesiastes
978-1-5154-4099-4 The Song of Solomon
978-1-5154-4100-7 The Book of the Prophet Isaiah
978-1-5154-4101-4 The Book of the Prophet Jeremiah
978-1-5154-4102-1 The Lamentations of Jeremiah
978-1-5154-4103-8 The Book of the Prophet Ezekiel
978-1-5154-4104-5 The Book of Daniel
978-1-5154-4105-2 The Book of Hosea
978-1-5154-4106-9 The Book of Joel
978-1-5154-4107-6 The Book of Amos

978-1-5154-4108-3 The Book of Obadiah
978-1-5154-4109-0 The Book of Jonah
978-1-5154-4110-6 The Book of Micah
978-1-5154-4111-3 The Book of Nahum
978-1-5154-4112-0 The Book of Habakkuk
978-1-5154-4113-7 The Book of Zephaniah
978-1-5154-4114-4 The Book of Haggai
978-1-5154-4115-1 The Book of Zechariah
978-1-5154-4116-8 The Book of Malachi

The New Testament

978-1-5154-4117-5 The Gospel According to Saint Matthew
978-1-5154-4118-2 The Gospel According to Saint Mark
978-1-5154-4119-9 The Gospel According to Saint Luke
978-1-5154-4120-5 The Gospel According to Saint John
978-1-5154-4121-2 The Acts of the Apostles
978-1-5154-4122-9 The Epistle of Paul the Apostle to the Romans
978-1-5154-4123-6 The First Epistle of Paul the Apostle to the Corinthians
978-1-5154-4124-3 The Second Epistle of Paul the Apostle to the Corinthians
978-1-5154-4125-0 The Epistle of Paul the Apostle to the Galatians
978-1-5154-4126-7 The Epistle of Paul the Apostle to the Ephesians
978-1-5154-4127-4 The Epistle of Paul the Apostle to the Philippians
978-1-5154-4128-1 The Epistle of Paul the Apostle to the Colossians
978-1-5154-4129-8 The First Epistle of Paul the Apostle to the Thessalonians
978-1-5154-4130-4 The Second Epistle of Paul the Apostle to the Thessalonians
978-1-5154-4131-1 The First Epistle of Paul the Apostle to Timothy
978-1-5154-4132-8 The Second Epistle of Paul the Apostle to Timothy
978-1-5154-4133-5 The Epistle of Paul the Apostle to Titus
978-1-5154-4134-2 The Epistle of Paul the Apostle to Philemon
978-1-5154-4135-9 The Epistle of Paul the Apostle to the Hebrews
978-1-5154-4136-6 The General Epistle of James

978-1-5154-4137-3 The First Epistle General of Peter
978-1-5154-4138-0 The Second General Epistle of Peter
978-1-5154-4139-7 The First Epistle General of John
978-1-5154-4140-3 The Second Epistle General of John
978-1-5154-4141-0 The Third Epistle General of John
978-1-5154-4142-7 The General Epistle of Jude
978-1-5154-4143-4 The Revelation of Saint John the Devine

CPSIA information can be obtained
at www.ICGtesting.com
Printed in the USA
LVHW110142130522
718699LV00001B/3

9 781515 440963